KB009663

THE ZACK FILES™

I'm Out of My Body....
Please Leave a Message

I'd like to thank my editors,
Jane O'Connor and Judy Donnelly,
who make the process of writing and revising
so much fun, and without whom
these books would not exist.

I also want to thank
Jennifer Dussling and Laura Driscoll
for their terrific ideas.

I'm Out of My Body . . . Please Leave a Message

Text copyright © 1997 by Dan Greenburg.
Illustration copyright © 1997 by Jack E. Davis.
All rights reserved.

First published in the United States by Grosset & Dunlap, Inc., a member of Penguin Putnam Books for
Young Readers under the title I'M OUT OF MY BODY . . . PLEASE LEAVE A MESSAGE.

No part of this publication may be reproduced, stored in a retrieval system, or transmitted, in any form or by any
means, graphic, electronic, or mechanical, including photocopying, taping, and recording, without prior written
permission from the publisher.
For information about permission, write to editor@longtailbooks.co.kr

This Korean and English edition was published by Longtail Books, Inc. in 2020 by arrangement with
Sheldon Fogelman Agency, Inc. through KCC(Korea Copyright Center Inc.), Seoul.

ISBN 979-11-86701-59-1 14740

Longtail Books

이 책의 저작권은 저자와의 계약으로 롱테일북스에 있습니다.
저작권법에 의해 한국 내에서 보호를 받는 저작물이므로 무단 전재와 복제를 금합니다.

I'm Out of My Body... Please Leave a Message

by Dan Greenburg
Illustrated by Jack E. Davis

For Judith, and for the real Zack,

with love—D.G.

Chapter 1

"Zack, have you ever been outside of your body?"

That's what my friend Spencer asked me. He was **sleep**ing **over** at my house. It was a pretty **weird** question. But I happen to know a lot about weird.

My great-grandpa died, and came back as a cat. A ghost named Wanda **trash**ed our apartment. Once I got an **electric shock** in science class, and I could read minds for a while. Oh, and there's a **parallel universe**[1] on the other side of the **medicine cabinet** in my bathroom. As I say, I know a lot about weird.

Anyway, this out-of-body[2] **stuff** was new to me. But it sounded kind of cool. My friend Spencer Sharp is the smartest kid in our class. Everybody knows it, **including** Spencer. I don't mean that the way it sounds. Spencer is very nice. And he**'s** always **up for** trying something new.

---

1 **parallel universe** 평행 우주. 공상 과학 소설이나 영화 등에서 사용하는 표현으로, 자신이 살고 있는 세계가 아닌 평행선 상에 위치한 또 다른 세계를 가리킨다.
2 **out-of-body** 유체 이탈. 사람의 영혼이 육체를 벗어나 육체 밖의 세상을 인지하는 경험을 말한다.

But I couldn't believe he knew something about weird stuff I didn't.

"How would you know if you were outside your body?" I asked him.

"Well, you'd be **float**ing in the air and looking down at yourself," he said.

"But if my eyes were in my body, what would I be looking down at it *with*?" I asked.

"With the eyes in your *astral*[3] body," he said.

"And what, **exact**ly, is an astral body?" I asked.

"It's the one inside your **regular** one.

---

3 **astral** ʻastralʼ은 영혼 또는 정신 세계와 관련된 경험이나 생각을 나타낼 때 사용하는 표현이다. ʻastral bodyʼ란 심령 현상에서 사람의 육체 속에 들어 있다고 여겨지는, 육체와 똑같이 생긴 유령 같은 존재를 가리키는 용어이다.

The one you can travel out-of-body with."

We were sitting on the floor in my bedroom, **lean**ing up against my **brand-new bunk** bed.

"How come you know about this stuff?" I asked.

Spencer pulled an old book out of his **backpack** and showed it to me. *Astral Travel for Beginners: Out-of-Body Journeys Through the World Mind.*

"I bought it at a **used**-book store," said Spencer. New York City has **load**s of used-book stores. And I **bet** Spencer has been in every one of them. "This book is from the 1960s," he said. "The hippie[4] days. It looks great."

"What's so great about traveling out-of-

body?"

"Well, it's faster than a plane. It's a whole lot cheaper. You don't have to stand in line to go through that stupid **metal detect**or. And you never lose your bags. What do you say we try it tonight?"

Just then my dad came into my room. My mom and dad are **divorce**d. I stay with each of them about half the time.

"Hey, guys," he said, "it's getting late. I know tonight's a Saturday. But I think it's time for bed. If you hurry, I'll let you talk in the dark for half an hour."

"OK," I said.

---

4 **hippie** (= hippy) 히피. 기성의 가치관 및 사회 제도를 부정하고 인간성 회복 등을 주장하며 자유로운 생활 양식을 추구하던 사람들 또는 그 문화를 말한다. 1960년대에 가장 유행하였다.

"Oh, I almost forgot," Dad said. "I just saw a mouse in the kitchen. So if you go in there for a **snack**, you may have **company**."

Dad left, and Spencer and I got into our **pajamas**. Then we climbed into bed. He got the top bunk because he was the guest. That's really why Dad got me the bunk bed—for **sleepover**s.

"So what do you say, Zack?" asked Spencer after we **turn**ed **off** the lights. "You want to try some out-of-body travel tonight?"

"I don't know," I said. "I guess so."

He **turn**ed **on** his **flashlight** and opened his out-of-body book. He began to read aloud: "**Get set** for a **groovy** time. First,

lie down with your eyes closed. Listen
to wind **chimes**,[5] if you have them. Be **at
one with** the universe. Then place your
left hand over your **forehead**. Right in the
middle. Aquarian Age[6] people call this the
third eye. Then place your right hand over
your **belly** button. . . ."

"It actually says belly button?"

"It says **navel**, OK? I wasn't sure you
knew the word."

Spencer doesn't usually act **superior**.
But I hate it when he does. "Thanks for
interpreting," I said.

---

5 **wind chimes** 풍경(風磬). 다양한 재료를 가지고 여러 모양으로 만들
   어 천장이나 건물 외관에 매다는 장식품. 바람의 흐름에 의해 고운 소리가
   난다.
6 **Aquarian Age** (= Age of Aquarius) 물병자리의 시대. 점성가들이 구
   분한 점성학적 시대 가운데 하나. 보통 1960년대에 시작되어 2000년간 지
   속된다고 여겨지며, 자유와 평화의 시대라고 일컬어진다.

"Now let your astral body slowly **seep** out of your real one . . . through your *navel*. OK?" Spencer **shot** me a look. Then he **went on** reading. "Seep out and float above you like **smoke**. . . ."

I tried doing what the book said. It didn't seem to be working.

"Are you doing all this too?" I asked.

"Of course," said Spencer. Spencer loves to say "of course."

"And is it working for you?" I asked.

"I don't know yet," he said.

That meant no. "Just keep trying," he said. "Sometimes it takes a while. Especially the first time."

"Have you done this a whole lot?" I asked.

"No, not that much."

"More than once?"

"Uh, no. Less."

We tried it for about an hour. Nothing happened. I told Spencer he must not be giving me the right **direction**s. He said I must not be following them right. But nothing was happening to him, either.

And then, finally, I felt something. A little **tickle** against the hand on my belly button. "Seep out. . . . Seep out," I kept telling my astral body.

A few minutes later I felt another tickle against my hand. This time it was like a breath. I opened my eyes. I was almost out of my body! But my leg was **stuck**. It felt like I was in quicksand.[7] I pulled

and pulled. Suddenly it **pop**ped free! And
then I was floating in the air! **Bob**bing up
against the **ceiling**!

---

7 **quicksand** 유사(流沙). 바람이나 물에 의해 아래로 흘러내리는 모래.
한번 들어가면 늪에 빠진 것처럼 헤어나오지 못한다.

Chapter 2

"Spencer!" I **yell**ed. "I'm on the **ceiling!**"

I **peer**ed down. I could see my own body. It was still lying on my bed. My eyes were closed. My left hand was still on my **forehead**. My right hand was still over my **belly** button.

Weird! I was seeing myself the way other people see me.

There was Spencer, lying on the top **bunk**. His eyes were closed. He wasn't moving. Was he sleeping, or what?

"Hey, Spencer!" I called. "Are you in there?"

"No!" said a voice right behind me. "I'm out here!"

I turned my head.

Spencer was **bob**bing against the ceiling right next to me! He looked about the same. Only you could sort of see through him. And he looked kind of **sparkly**.

"We did it!" I said. "We actually got out of our bodies!"

"Of course," said Spencer. Just like he did it every night of his life.

This was **amazing**. My body felt lighter

than air. My body felt like it had no **weight**. My body felt like I had no body.

Moving around was fun. I found out that if I **breathe**d out, I started to **sink**. But if I breathed in, I rose. To go forward, all I had to do was move my arms and legs, like I was swimming. Swimming in the air. Just for the fun of it, I did a loop-the-loop.[1]

"This is very cool," I said.

"So where would you like to travel to?" Spencer asked.

"I don't know," I said. "Where could we go?"

"Anywhere we want," said Spencer. He

---

1 loop-the-loop 공중제비. 두 손을 땅에 짚고 두 다리를 공중으로 쳐들어서 반대 방향으로 넘는 재주.

had a big sparkling **grin** on his face.

"How about into my dad's study?" I said.

"I was thinking more like Egypt,[2]" said Spencer.

Spencer had just done a **geography** project on Egypt. He built a pyramid[3] out of 743 sugar **cube**s. It was pretty amazing.

"What would we do in Egypt?" I asked.

"I don't know," said Spencer. "Go down the Nile.[4] See the pyramids."

"Cool!" I said. "But will it take us a

---

2 **Egypt** 이집트. 아프리카 대륙 동북부 나일강 유역에 있는 공화국으로 인류 문명 발상지 가운데 하나이다.

3 **pyramid** 피라미드. 돌이나 벽돌을 쌓아 만든 사각뿔 모양의 거대한 건조물. 기원전 2700년에서 기원전 2500년 사이에 이집트나 에티오피아 등에서 건조되었으며 주로 왕이나 왕족의 무덤으로 만들어졌다.

4 **Nile** 나일강. 아프리카 동북부를 흐르는 강으로 세계에서 가장 긴 강이다. 길이가 약 6,700킬로미터에 달한다.

long time to get there?"

"Probably," said Spencer. "Egypt is more than 5,000 miles[5] away."

"Well, we have to be back by morning," I said. "**Otherwise** my dad will worry. Let's pick something closer to home. How about the Bronx Zoo?[6]"

"The zoo is fine," said Spencer.

I **float**ed to the door. It was closed. I couldn't open it. I couldn't even **grip** the **doorknob**. I floated to the window. It was closed too.

"How are we ever going to get out of here?" I asked.

---

5 **mile** 거리의 단위 마일. 1마일은 약 1.6킬로미터이다. (5,000마일은 약 8,046킬로미터이다.)

6 **Bronx Zoo** 브롱크스 동물원. 미국 뉴욕주(州) 브롱크스(Bronx) 지구에 있으며, 뉴욕 동물원이라고도 부른다. 미국에서 가장 큰 동물원이다.

"What if you go through the wall?" said Spencer.

"And just how do I do that?" I asked.

"Like this," said Spencer.

He put his hands together over his head. He did a **scissors** kick[7] with his legs. He **dove** into my bedroom wall. His hands **disappear**ed. Then his head. Then the rest of him. Spencer **slid** through the wall like it was Jell-O.[8]

Awesome!

"Hey! Wait for me!" I called out.

I put my hands together and pushed

---

7 scissors kick 가위 차기. 수영에서 사용하는 발차기이다. 가위질을 하는 것처럼 무릎을 벌렸다가 다시 다리를 끌어당겨 크게 바깥쪽으로 차는 동작이다.

8 Jell-O 젤로. 젤라틴에 과일즙, 설탕을 넣어 굳혀 만든 투명한 디저트용 젤리로, 미국 크라프트(Kraft)사에서 만든 제품의 상표명이다.

off. My head went through the wall. I saw **flash**es of wood and **brick**. I felt nothing.

And then I was outside.

Yikes!

I was thirty **stories** up!

There was nothing **underneath** me but air! Far below me were the **tiny** lights of the city.

Help!

Chapter 3

I panicked. The air **rush**ed out of my
lungs. I began to fall. Then I remembered
to **breathe** in. And I floated back up.
Spencer was waiting for me, **giggling**.

"So, are we going to the zoo?" he asked.

"Follow me," I said.

We left Dad's building on East 52nd
Street. We flew **uptown** . . . over the tops of

tall buildings . . . over Park Avenue[1] . . .
over lines of cars going both ways . . .
and then over Central Park.[2] I felt like
Superman.[3] I could almost hear the music
from the *Superman* movies.

"Is this great, or what?" Spencer
shouted.

"The greatest!" I shouted back.

Soon we were flying over the Bronx
Zoo.

"Ladies and gentlemen," I said, "this is
your **captain**. We **are about to land** at the

---

1 **Park Avenue** 파크 애비뉴. 미국 뉴욕시의 맨해튼(Manhattan)에 있는
   번화한 거리이다.
2 **Central Park** 센트럴 파크. 미국 뉴욕시의 맨해튼 중심부에 있는 공원.
   공원에 인공 호수와 연못, 아이스링크, 동물원 등이 있어 수많은 관광객이
   찾는 명소이다.
3 **Superman** 슈퍼맨. 미국의 대표적인 만화 제목이자 그 주인공. 초인적
   인 힘을 지닌 영웅으로 하늘을 나는 것이 그의 능력 가운데 하나이다. 애
   니메이션, 영화 등으로도 제작되어 많은 인기를 얻었다.

Bronx Zoo. Please make sure that your seat belts are **secure**ly **fasten**ed. And your seat backs and **tray** tables must be in the **upright** and **lock**ed position."

We floated down toward the ground.

"Ladies and gentlemen," I **went on**, "we have arrived at the Bronx Zoo. We hope you have a **pleasant** evening. We thank you for flying Out-of-Body Airlines. For those of you in our **Frequent** Flier program,[4] tonight's **flight** is **worth** fifteen miles.[5]"

The zoo was closed. There were no people—**except** for Spencer and me. But,

---

4 **Frequent Flier Program** 항공사에서 비행기를 이용하는 승객들에게 사용한 총거리에 비례하여 제공하는 여러 가지 혜택.

5 **mile** 비행기를 이용하는 승객들에게 적립되는 탑승 마일리지. 보통 이용한 총 거리에 비례하여 적립된다.

come to think of it, I'm not sure we really **count**ed as people. It was very dark. And far away you could hear a wolf or something **howl**ing.

"It's a lot **creepier** here at night," said Spencer.

I **nod**ded. "But as long as we're here, let's go see the lions," I said. I**'m crazy about** lions.

We went to the lion area. We didn't see any lions.

"So, where are they?" I asked.

"In bed, I **bet**," said Spencer. "It's nighttime."

"Then they must be right inside that **cave**," I said. "Let's go and have a look."

"Zack, are you crazy?"

"Spencer, we're out of our bodies."

"And you're **out of your mind**."

"But if we're not in our bodies," I said, "they can't hurt us. Right?"

Spencer seemed to see the **logic** of that.

"C'mon!" I said.

We floated into the cave. You couldn't see a thing. But you could hear the **snoring**. It was a weird sound. A **bunch** of **huge pussycat**s, snoring in the dark. Then one of them **cough**ed. OK, it was half a cough and half a **roar**.

"Zack," Spencer **whisper**ed right near me, "this is a really **dumb** idea."

"Why?"

"Why? Because. They might wake up. And they might just decide to **bite** our astral **butt**s off."

"Hmmmm. Maybe you**'ve got a point** there," I said.

With me leading the way, we floated back toward the cave **entrance**.

Our astral eyes must have gotten **used** to the dark. Or maybe it was just brighter at the cave entrance. Because when we got there, we didn't have any trouble seeing the huge lion that was standing in front of us.

It was the biggest lion I had ever seen. Or maybe I'd just never seen a lion up close before.

"M-maybe he c-can't see us," Spencer whispered.

I raised my hand and **wave**d it a little.

The lion didn't seem to **notice**. I waved both my arms. The lion opened his mouth. And **yawn**ed.

"He *can't* see us!" I said.

So I moved toward the lion.

Weird! Now the lion took a step backward.

I went a little nearer. The lion moved back farther.

"Wow! He **sense**s we're here," Spencer whispered.

"And *he's* afraid of *us*!" I said out loud.

The lion took a step forward. And roared.

"OK," I said, "so he's not afraid of us."

"We should get out of here," Spencer whispered.

"Spencer," I said, "follow me!"

I backed up several feet.[6] I put my hands together and **dove** toward an open space at the lion's right.

Oops! The lion moved to the right. And opened his mouth. Wide.

I tried to stop. I couldn't. I dove straight into the lion's mouth, with Spencer right behind me.

---

6 **feet** 길이의 단위 피트. 1피트는 약 30.48센티미터이다.

Chapter 4

We went through the lion's mouth. We **slid** right through his body. We were free!

A second later we were **zoom**ing up and away from the Bronx Zoo.

"Where are we going now?" Spencer called.

"You'll see!" I said.

The **amusement park** at Coney Island[1] in Brooklyn[2] was as dark and **desert**ed as the zoo. The **hump**s of roller-coaster[3] hills looked like **dinosaur skeleton**s. It was cool, in a very **weird** way.

Spencer wanted to go on the roller coaster right away. Of course, the cars weren't running. So we decided to go on it *without* the cars. Going down the hills **headfirst** was really fun. But unless you're out of your body, I don't **suggest** you try it.

Our next stop was the **Statue** of

---

1 **Coney Island** 코니아일랜드. 미국 뉴욕시의 브루클린 남쪽에 있는, 놀이공원과 해변이 있는 휴양지이다.
2 **Brooklyn** 브루클린. 미국 뉴욕시의 다섯 자치구 중 하나로 롱아일랜드 (Long Island)의 서쪽 끝에 위치한다. 뉴욕시에서 가장 인구가 많은 자치구이다.
3 **roller-coaster** (=roller coaster) 롤러코스터. 지상보다 높은 곳에 설치된 경사진 레일 위를 아주 빠르게 달리면서 오르내리도록 만들어진 놀이기구.

Liberty.[4] I've always wanted to go to the very top. But I never felt like standing in line or climbing up all those stairs. Spencer and I flew to the top of the **torch**. It was an **awesome** view.

Then I got an idea. I flew right under the Statue of Liberty's nose.

"Guess what I am!" I **yell**ed to Spencer.

"I give up."

"An astral **booger!**"

After that we headed **uptown** again. On Broadway[5] near Times Square,[6] we saw a long line **stretch**ing around the **block**.

---

4 **Statue of Liberty** 자유의 여신상. 미국 뉴욕항의 리버티섬(Liberty Island)에 세워진 거대한 조각상. 1886년에 미국 독립 100주년을 기념하여 프랑스가 선물한 것이다.

5 **Broadway** 브로드웨이. 미국 뉴욕시의 맨해튼을 남북으로 비스듬하게 가로지르는 큰길. 보통 지리적인 개념보다는 미국의 연극·뮤지컬계를 일컫는 대명사로 사용되고 있다.

Terminator 3000[7] had just opened. None of our parents wanted us to see it. About a **million** people get killed in all kinds of **horrible** ways.

"Now's our chance!" said Spencer.

So down we flew. We went right through all the people in line. And, of course, we didn't have to pay!

The popcorn smelled great. I went over to **help myself to** a bag. But then it **hit** me. I couldn't eat any. **Bummer**!

Spencer was looking at a **bunch** of video games in the **lobby**. There were lots

---

6 **Times Square** 타임스 스퀘어. 미국 뉴욕시 맨해튼 중심부에 있는 거리. 브로드웨이와 42번가가 교차하는 거리로 극장과 식당 등이 즐비한 번화가로 유명하다.

7 **Terminator 3000** 1994년에 개봉한 SF 영화 터미네이터(Terminator)를 기반으로 한 3D 애니메이션 영화로, 제작이 기획되었다가 무산되었다.

of cool ones. But every time we tried to hold on to the **control**s, our astral hands just **slip**ped right through them.

So we waited for the movie to begin. Usually I get **stuck** behind some guy who's about seven feet tall. This time, no problem. Spencer and I had a perfect view from up near the **ceiling**.

The trouble was, the movie was way **scarier** than we thought it would be. I looked at Spencer. He looked at me.

"I think we ought to go back home now," I said.

"Why?" said Spencer.

"Because," I said. "I need my sleep. If I don't get home and get some sleep, I'm going to be a **mess** tomorrow."

"You *are* home **asleep**," said Spencer. "At least your body is. The rest of you can **stay out** as late as you like."

"I still think we ought to go home," I said.

"Uh, OK," said Spencer.

Little did I know the scariest part of our **adventure** was waiting for us there!

Chapter 5

By the time we got back to my dad's apartment and **slid** through the wall into my room, it was really late. I wanted to go to bed. Even though I didn't have to. **Weird**, huh?

"OK, Spencer," I said, "how do we get back into our bodies?"

"There are several ways to do that," he

said.

"Which one should we use?"

"Uh, probably the one the book says."

"And what does the book say?"

"Well, let's see here."

He **float**ed over to the book, which was beside his body on the top **bunk**.

"Well?" I said.

"There seems to be a little problem," he said.

"What kind of a little problem?"

"The book is opened to page thirteen," he said. "That's the page for getting out of our bodies. The **direction**s for getting back *in* are on the next page. On page fourteen."

"Well, turn the page."

Spencer looked at me.

"Oh, no," I said. I **smack**ed my astral **forehead** with my astral hand. "You can't turn the page."

"I could if I were in my body," he said.

"If you were in your body, you wouldn't *have* to," I said.

"Right."

"What do we do if we can't get back into our bodies?" I said.

Spencer **shrug**ged **nervous**ly. That **spook**ed me. Spencer always knows the answer to any question. But not this time.

"Maybe Dad can help us," I said.

I swam through my bedroom door and floated into Dad's bedroom. Spencer followed me.

Dad was fast **asleep**. One leg was hanging down off the bed. His eyes were closed. His mouth was open. And he was kind of **drool**ing onto his **pillow**.

"Dad!" I **yell**ed. "Wake up!"

He **went on** sleeping.

I floated down to his head. I put my **lip**s right up to his ear.

"Dad! Wake up! We're in trouble!"

Dad is a very **sound** sleeper. He didn't move an **inch**.

"Spencer," I said, "Dad is not waking up."

"I can see that," said Spencer. He was floating right beside me. He thought for a moment. Then he said, "What if we go to Mrs. Coleman-Levin's house?"

"What good would that do?" I asked.

Mrs. Coleman-Levin is our science and **homeroom** teacher.[1] She's also kind of weird. She keeps a pig's **brain** in a **jar** on her desk. She wears work **boot**s, even for **dressy** parties. And on weekends she does autopsies[2] at the **morgue**. That means she cuts up dead bodies to see what they died of. Ugh!

"She knows about lots of weird **stuff**," said Spencer. "Maybe she can help. And I happen to know she **stay**s **up** till **dawn**."

I didn't have a better idea. So I said, "Why not?"

---

1 **homeroom teacher** 담임 선생님. 홈룸(homeroom)은 미국 학교에서 학생들이 출석 확인이나 종례 등을 위해 모이는 교실을 말한다.
2 **autopsy** 부검(剖檢). 시신을 해부하여 사망의 원인을 검사하는 일.

Spencer knew the way to Mrs. Coleman-Levin's house. He got **extra credit** one vacation for catching live **insect**s to **feed** to her **huge** Venus fly trap.³ He led the way across town to her apartment.

Mrs. Coleman-Levin's apartment was very cool. It looked like a rain forest.⁴ It had a huge palm tree⁵ and lots of **tropical** plants and hanging **vine**s and stuff like that. It even had a little **waterfall**. And, of course, the Venus fly trap.

We found Mrs. Coleman-Levin's room.

---

3 **Venus fly trap** 파리지옥풀. 습지에서 자라는 벌레잡이 식물. 잎 가장 자리에 가시 같은 긴 털이 있어서 벌레가 닿으면 잎을 급히 닫아 잡아먹는 다.

4 **rain forest** 우림(雨林). 연중 우량이 많고 습윤하게 유지되며 수목이 잘 자라 울창한 밀림이 조성된 숲.

5 **palm tree** 야자나무. 높이 10~30미터의 상록수로 잎은 깃모양이다. 나무와 열매를 모두 사용할 수 있어 경제성이 높다.

She was in bed. Fast asleep. With her work boots on.

"Spencer, I thought you said she stays up till dawn," I said. "It isn't dawn yet."

"Then I was wrong," said Spencer.

"Or else she's still up," said another voice.

The voice had come from above. We looked up.

Mrs. Coleman-Levin was sitting **cross-legged** near the **ceiling**!

Chapter 6

"**M**rs. Coleman-Levin! You're out of your body!" I shouted.

"A **splendid observation**, Zack," she said.

"But how did you do that?" asked Spencer.

"How did *you?*" she said.

"We learned from a book," I said.

"Good place to learn," she said. "Where have you gone since you've been out?"

"To the Bronx Zoo," I said. "And Coney Island. And the **Statue** of **Liberty**. And the movies."

"Sounds like you've had a pretty full night," she said.

"We have," said Spencer.

"Why did you come to see me?"

"We don't know how to get back into our bodies," Spencer said. "We thought you might know."

"I *do* know," she said.

"Great!" I said. "Will you tell us?"

"Of course not," she said with a smile.

"Why not?" I said.

"Because. If I tell you, you won't learn

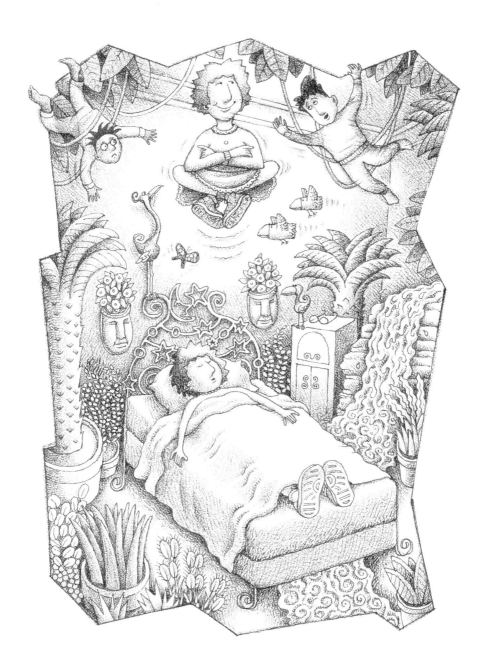

anything. If you **figure** it **out** for yourself, you will."

"We could find out from the book," said Spencer. "But the book is opened to page thirteen. And the directions for getting back in are on page fourteen. And we can't turn the page."

"Then I **suggest** you do some **experiment**ing," she said. Mrs. Coleman-Levin **is big on** experimenting. "And I **bet** you'll **come up with** a **solution**."

Mrs. Coleman-Levin **wave**d good-bye. I guess we **were supposed to** leave.

"Won't you tell us anything at all?" I asked.

"Why,[1] certainly," she said. "I'll tell you that no one who's in his or her body can see you. Or hear you. But you both are smart boys. So put your astral minds to work. Because if you're not inside your bodies and in class **prompt**ly at 8:30 on Monday morning, I'm going to have to **mark** you **absent**. And I would hate to do that!"

1 **why** 여기에서는 이유를 묻거나 말할 때 쓰는 의문사 또는 관계사가 아닌 '어머', '아니'라는 뜻의 감탄사로 쓰였다.

Chapter 7

By the time we got back to Dad's apartment, it was Sunday morning. Both Spencer and I were tired of being out of our bodies. As much fun as it is passing through walls and flying over the city, it's nice to be able to **scratch** your neck. Or **snuggle** down in bed. Or eat a bagel[1] and cream cheese[2] for breakfast. I never thought I'd miss simple **stuff** like that.

We swam into my room. There we were—on the top and bottom **bunk**s. Just where we left us.

"What do we do now?" I asked.

"I don't know," said Spencer. "Why don't you try climbing into your body through your mouth?"

I **float**ed over to my body.

"My mouth is closed," I said.

"Well, *that's* **unusual**," said Spencer.

I **glare**d at him.

Spencer floated up to his body and looked at it.

---

1 **bagel** 베이글. 밀가루, 이스트, 물, 소금만으로 만든, 가운데 구멍이 뚫린 둥글고 딱딱한 빵.

2 **cream cheese** 크림치즈. 크림과 우유를 섞어 만든 치즈. 숙성하지 않아 부드러우며 빵에 발라 먹거나 다양한 요리에 사용한다.

"Mine is closed too," he said. "Hey, why don't you try to **fit** yourself in through your **nostril**?"

I looked at my body and shook my head.

"I couldn't fit more than a finger in there," I said.

"I've already seen you do that," said Spencer.

I gave him a **punch** on his astral arm. It passed right through his arm and out the other side.

Suddenly something small and **furry scamper**ed across the top bunk. Then it ran down the wall and stopped on the bottom bunk.

"**Yikes**!" I said. "It's the mouse!"

"You're afraid of a *mouse?*" said Spencer. "You're a guy who **dove** into a lion's mouth."

"It just surprised me, that's all," I said. "Spencer, what if we can't **figure out** how to get back into our bodies?"

"Then Monday morning Mrs. Coleman-Levin will **mark** us **absent**," said Spencer.

"**Never mind** Mrs. Coleman-Levin," I said. "In an hour or so, my dad's going to come in here to wake us for breakfast. If he can't wake us, what's he going to think?"

"That we're **unconscious**," said Spencer.

I **nod**ded. Dad was not going to **react** well to that.

"We've got to figure something out," I

said. "Spencer, you're the **genius**. Think of something!"

"Hmmmm. Maybe we should try the **Scientific Method**,[3]" Spencer **suggest**ed. The Scientific Method is something else Mrs. Coleman-Levin is always talking about. It's the way real **scientist**s **solve** problems.

"We **might as well**," I said.

"Step one in the Scientific Method is to **observe**," said Spencer. "Well, I observe that there's no way we can turn the page on that book ourselves."

So far I was with him.

---

3 **Scientific Method** 과학적 방법. 현상을 설명하는 가설을 세우고, 이 가설에 의한 예측이 들어맞는지를 알아보기 위해 실험을 진행하여 문제를 해결하는 방법.

"Step two is to **form** a **theory**," Spencer **went on**.

"OK," I said.

"I have a theory that we could get somebody to turn that page for us," said Spencer.

"And who, **exact**ly, did you **have in mind**?" I said.

Just then the mouse reappeared from under my bed. It scampered across the **rug**.

"The mouse, of course," said Spencer.

"The mouse?" I said.

Spencer saw I looked **doubtful**.

"Zack, animals can't see us," he said. "But the lion did seem to **sense** us."

"True," I said. "But so what?"

"Well," said Spencer, "maybe we can **corner** the mouse by the book. Maybe we can get him to run across the page and turn it over."

Hmmmm. Well, it was a **long shot**. But for now it was all we had.

"OK," I said. "Let's **go for** it."

"Step three: Test the theory," said Spencer.

So we did. The mouse was starting to **nibble** on my teddy bear.[4] I didn't like that at all. I floated toward my teddy bear. The mouse looked up.

"Hi, mouse," I said. I don't know why I was talking to a mouse, but I was. "You

---

4 **teddy bear** 테디 베어. 장난감 곰 인형으로, 미국의 26대 대통령 테어도어 루스벨트(Theodore Roosevelt)의 애칭을 따서 만들었다.

can't see us, but we're here. We're boys.
Boys who like mice. We need you to do us
a **favor**. Just go up to the top bunk. And
run across that book. And turn the page
for us."

The mouse seemed **confuse**d. He
seemed **spook**ed. He backed away from
me.

Good! He was moving in the right
direction. He ran up to the top bunk.
Toward the book. But then he ran past the
book and down the wall to the floor. And
then he **disappear**ed.

"Darn![5]" I said.

"**So much for** the Scientific Method,"

---

5 **darn** 'damn(빌어먹을)'을 순화한 단어로, 못마땅하거나 짜증스러울 때
쓰는 표현.

said Spencer.

Just then my bedroom door opened. Dad stuck his head in. He looked toward the bunk beds.

Boy,[6] was I glad to see him!

"Dad!" I shouted, forgetting he couldn't hear us. "We're in trouble! We really need your help!"

"Aw, they look so cute **asleep**," said my dad.

"No, Dad! We're not asleep! We're not cute! We're up here!" I shouted.

"Good morning, gentlemen," said my dad. "Who'd like waffles[7] with strawberry

---

6 **boy** 여기에서는 '소년'이라는 뜻이 아니라, '맙소사!' 또는 '어머나!'라는
   의미로 놀람이나 기쁨 등을 나타내는 표현으로 쓰였다.
7 **waffle** 와플. 밀가루, 달걀, 우유, 설탕 등을 섞은 반죽을 격자 무늬 틀
   에 넣어 구운 것으로, 잼이나 버터 등을 얹어 먹는다.

jam for breakfast?"

"Dad!" I said. "You have *got* to help us!"

Dad walked over to the bed. He **gently** shook my body by the shoulders.

"Wake up, Zack," he said.

"Dad! I'm not asleep! I'm just not inside my body!"

"Zack?"

Dad looked **puzzle**d.

"Dad! How can I **get through to** you?"

"Zack, what's wrong with you? Are you **faking**?"

Dad stood up and **poke**d Spencer. Then Dad saw the book. The out-of-body book. He picked it up and looked at it.

"What the . . . ? *Astral Travel for Beginners*?"

"Yes! That's right! He's going to figure it out, Spencer! My dad is going to figure it out!"

Dad took a fast **peek** inside the book.

"Hmmmm," he said. "Did you guys find a way to leave your bodies?"

"We did!" I **scream**ed. "Yes! That's exactly what we did!"

"If you'd left your bodies," said my dad, "you'd probably be **invisible**. . . ."

"Yes, Dad! Yes!" I screamed. "We are!"

"You might even be floating right in front of my face. And I couldn't see you. . . ."

"Yes!" I screamed. "That's right!"

"You might even be talking to me. And I couldn't even hear you. . . . "

"We are, Dad! We are!"

"Hi, Zack," said my dad. But he was **facing** the wrong direction. He was talking to the air. Then he shook his head.

"Nah!" he said. "These guys probably **stay**ed **up** till **dawn**, talking. I'll just let them sleep some more. I'll come back in a few minutes."

Dad **toss**ed the book on the floor and walked to the door.

"No, Dad! Don't leave!"

The door closed behind Dad.

"Well," I said, "at least he'll be back in a few minutes."

"Yes," said Spencer. "And when we still don't wake up, he's going to **freak**."

That was true. Poor Dad. He'd think we were both in a coma[8] or something.

"Spencer, what are we going to do?"

Spencer didn't answer me. He was **staring** at the book.

"Zack!" shouted Spencer. "Look!"

"What?"

"Page fourteen," he said. "When your dad threw the book down, the page turned. I can just **make out** the directions."

"Let me see," I said.

"**Better yet**," he said, "I'll read them to you. Do exactly as I say!"

"OK," I said.

"First," said Spencer, reading aloud,

---

8 **coma** 혼수상태. 의식을 잃고 인사불성이 되는 일. 부르거나 흔들어서 깨워도 정신을 차리지 못하고 외부의 자극에 대한 반응이나 반사 작용도 보이지 않는 의학적 상태를 말한다.

"did you have a totally **groovy** time out of your body? Did you feel totally **at one with** the **universe**? Are you ready now to re-enter your body?"

"Yes!" I shouted.

"Then get **parallel** with your body," Spencer continued. "Float just a few inches above it. . . ."

"OK," I said.

I floated over to the lower bunk. I got parallel with my body. I floated a few inches above it.

"Make sure the hands of your astral body are in the same place as those of your real body," Spencer read. "Your left hand on your **forehead**, over your third eye. Your right hand on your **navel** . . ."

"OK," I said.

"Listen to your wind **chime**s," he read.

"Forget the wind chimes!" I said.

"Now, close your eyes and picture a big **funnel** in your navel. . . ." he continued.

"OK," I said.

"**Pour** yourself through that funnel," Spencer read, "right into your navel. Just like a **bucket** of sand."

"OK," I said.

I closed my eyes. I pictured the funnel. I pictured pouring myself into it like a bucket of sand.

Whoosh! In I went!

I felt my body start to come alive again! Parts of me began to **tingle**. First my **toe**s and fingers. Then my **wrist**s and **ankle**s.

Then my legs and arms. Then my **chest** and **lung**s. And finally my head and face.

I opened up my eyes. I was back in my body!

"I'm back in!" I shouted.

I looked around for Spencer. He was gone.

"Spencer!" I called. "Where are you?"

And then I **realize**d: I was back in my body. I could no longer see anybody who was out of theirs.

I climbed the **ladder** to the top bunk.

Spencer looked like he was fast asleep. If he wasn't back in his body, then where was he?

"Spencer!" I shouted. "Speak to me!"

Suddenly Spencer's eyes **snap**ped open.

"What do you want me to say?" said Spencer.

I **giggle**d. Just then Dad came back into my bedroom.

"Well, well, well, you're finally **awake**," he said. "What time did you guys get to sleep?"

Spencer and I looked at each other.

"It's a long story, sir," said Spencer.

"Then tell me," said my dad. "I'm a writer. I love long stories."

So we all went in to breakfast. Let me tell you. Waffles with strawberry jam had never tasted so good!

That night Dad didn't have to **nag** me about going to bed. I wanted to get to school early on Monday.

I couldn't wait for Mrs. Coleman-Levin to see Spencer and me.

No way was she going to mark us absent!

THE ZACK FILES™

I'm Out of My Body... Please Leave a Message

by Dan Greenburg
Illustrated by Jack E. Davis

CONTENTS

**평범한 소년이 겪는 기상천외하고 흥미로운 모험을 그린 이야기,
잭 파일스!**

『잭 파일스(The Zack Files)』 시리즈는 뉴욕에 사는 평범한 소년, 잭이 겪는 때로는 으스스하고, 때로는 우스꽝스러운 모험을 담고 있습니다. 저자 댄 그린버그(Dan Greenburg)는 자신의 아들 잭에게서 영감을 받아서 그를 주인공으로 한 이야기를 떠올렸고, 초자연적인 현상에 대한 자신의 관심과 잭과 같은 아이들이 독서에 흥미를 갖길 바라는 마음을 담아서 책을 썼습니다.
그렇기 때문에 『잭 파일스』 시리즈는 누구나 한 번은 들어 본 기괴한 이야기를 아이들이 재미있게 읽을 수 있도록 흥미진진하게 소개합니다. 이 시리즈는 현재까지 총 30권의 책이 출간될 정도로 아이들의 호기심을 불러 일으켰고, 심지어 TV 드라마로도 제작되어 많은 관심과 사랑을 받았습니다.
이러한 이유로 『잭 파일스』 시리즈는 '엄마표 영어'를 하는 부모님과 초보 영어 학습자라면 반드시 읽어야 하는 영어 원서로 자리 잡았습니다. 간결한 어휘로 재치 있게 풀어 쓴 이야기는 원서 읽기에 두려움을 느끼는 학습자에게도 영어로 책을 읽는 재미를 선사할 것입니다.

퀴즈와 단어장, 그리고 번역까지 담긴 알찬 구성의 워크북!

이 책은 영어원서 『잭 파일스』 시리즈에, 탁월한 학습 효과를 거둘 수 있도록 다양한 콘텐츠를 덧붙인 책입니다.
• 영어원서: 본문에 나온 어려운 어휘에 볼드 처리가 되어 있어 단어를 더욱 분명히 인지하며 자연스럽게 암기하게 됩니다.
• 단어장: 원서에 나온 어려운 어휘가 '한영'은 물론 '영영' 의미까지 완벽하게 정리되어 있으며, 반복되는 단어까지 표시하여 자연스럽게 복습이 되도록 구성했습니다.
• 번역: 영어와 비교할 수 있도록 직역에 가까운 번역을 담았습니다. 원서 읽기에 익숙하지 않은 초보 학습자도 어려움 없이 내용을 파악할 수 있습니다.
• 퀴즈: 챕터별로 내용을 확인하는 이해력 점검 퀴즈가 들어 있습니다.

『잭 파일스』, 이렇게 읽어보세요!

● **단어 암기는 이렇게!** 처음 리딩을 시작하기 전, 해당 챕터에 나오는 단어를 눈으로 쭉 훑어봅니다. 모르는 단어는 좀 더 주의 깊게 보되, 손으로 쓰면서 완벽하게 암기할 필요는 없습니다. 본문을 읽으면서 이 단어를 다시 만나게 되는데, 그 과정에서 단어의 쓰임새와 어감을 자연스럽게 익히게 됩니다. 이렇게 책을 읽은 후에, 단어를 다시 한 번 복습하세요. 복습할 때는 중요하다고 생각하는 단어들을 손으로 쓰면서 꼼꼼하게 외우는 것도 좋습니다. 이런 방식으로 책을 읽다보면, 많은 단어를 빠르고 부담 없이 익히게 됩니다.

● **리딩할 때는 리딩에만 집중하자!** 원서를 읽는 중간 중간 모르는 단어가 나온다고 워크북을 들춰보거나, 곧바로 번역을 찾아보는 것은 매우 좋지 않은 습관입니다. 모르는 단어나 이해가 가지 않는 문장이 나온다고 해도 펜으로 가볍게 표시만 해두고, 전체적인 맥락을 잡아가며 빠르게 읽어나가세요. 리딩을 할 때는 속도에 대한 긴장감을 잃지 않으면서 리딩에만 집중하는 것이 좋습니다. 모르는 단어와 문장은, 리딩이 끝난 후에 한꺼번에 정리하는 '리뷰' 시간을 갖습니다. 리뷰를 할 때는 번역은 물론 단어장과 사전도 꼼꼼하게 확인하면서 왜 이해가 되지 않았는지 확인해 봅니다.

● **번역 활용은 이렇게!** 이해가 가지 않는 문장은 번역을 통해서 그 의미를 파악할 수 있습니다. 하지만 한국어와 영어는 정확히 1:1 대응이 되지 않기 때문에 번역을 활용하는 데에도 지혜가 필요합니다. 의역이 된 부분까지 억지로 의미를 대응해서 암기하려고 하기보다, 어떻게 그런 의미가 만들어진 것인지 추측하면서 번역은 참고 자료로 활용하는 것이 좋습니다.

● **2~3번 반복해서 읽자!** 영어 초보자라면 2~3회 반복해서 읽을 것을 추천합니다. 초보자일수록 처음 읽을 때는 생소한 단어와 스토리 때문에 내용 파악에 급급할 수밖에 없습니다. 하지만 일단 내용을 파악한 후에 다시 읽으면 어휘와 문장 구조 등 다른 부분까지 관찰하면서 조금 더 깊이 있게 읽을 수 있고, 그 과정에서 리딩 속도도 빨라지고 리딩 실력을 더 확고하게 다지게 됩니다.

- **'시리즈'로 꾸준히 읽자!** 한 작가의 책을 시리즈로 읽는 것 또한 영어 실력 향상에 큰 도움이 됩니다. 같은 등장인물이 다시 나오기 때문에 내용 파악이 더 수월할 뿐 아니라, 작가가 사용하는 어휘와 표현들도 자연스럽게 반복되기 때문에 탁월한 복습 효과까지 얻을 수 있습니다. 『잭 파일스』 시리즈는 현재 6권, 총 31,441단어 분량이 출간되어 있습니다. 시리즈를 꾸준히 읽다 보면 영어 실력도 자연스럽게 향상될 것입니다.

영어원서 본문 구성

내용이 담긴 본문입니다.
원어민이 읽는 일반 원서와 같은 텍스트지만, 암기해야 할 중요 어휘는 볼드체로 표시되어 있습니다. 이 어휘들은 지금 들고 계신 워크북에 챕터별로 정리되어 있습니다.

학습 심리학 연구 결과에 따르면, 한 단어씩 따로 외우는 단어 암기는 거의 효과가 없다고 합니다. 대신 단어를 제대로 외우기 위해서는 문맥(Context) 속에서 단어를 암기해야 하며, 한 단어 당 문맥 속에서 15번 이상 마주칠 때 완벽하게 암기할 수 있다고 합니다.

이 책의 본문은 중요 어휘를 볼드로 강조하여, 문맥 속의 단어들을 더 확실히 인지(Word Cognition in Context)하도록 돕고 있습니다. 또한 대부분의 중요한 단어는 다른 챕터에서도 반복해서 등장하기 때문에 이 책을 읽는 것만으로도 자연스럽게 어휘력을 향상시킬 수 있습니다.

또한 본문에는 내용 이해를 돕기 위해 '각주'가 첨가되어 있습니다. 각주는 굳이 암기할 필요는 없지만, 알아 두면 내용을 더 깊이 있게 이해할 수 있어 원서를 읽는 재미가 배가됩니다.

THE ZACK FILES

워크북(Workbook)의 구성

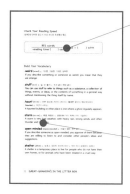

Check Your Reading Speed

해당 챕터의 단어 수가 기록되어 있어, 리딩 속도를 측정할 수 있습니다. 특히 리딩 속도를 중시하는 독자는 유용하게 사용할 수 있습니다.

Build Your Vocabulary

본문에 볼드 표시되어 있는 단어가 정리되어 있습니다. 리딩 전, 후에 반복해서 보면 원서를 더욱 쉽게 읽을 수 있고, 어휘력도 빠르게 향상됩니다.

단어는 〈빈도 − 스펠링 − 발음기호 − 품사 − 한국어 뜻 − 영어 뜻〉 순서로 표기되어 있으며 빈도 표시(★)가 많을수록 필수 어휘입니다. 반복해서 등장하는 단어는 빈도 대신 '복습'으로 표기되어 있습니다. 품사는 아래와 같이 표기했습니다.

n.명사 | a.형용사 | ad.부사 | v.동사

conj.접속사 | prep.전치사 | int.감탄사 | idiom 숙어 및 관용구

Comprehension Quiz

간단한 퀴즈를 통해 읽은 내용에 대한 이해력을 점검해 볼 수 있습니다.

번역

영문과 비교할 수 있도록 최대한 직역에 가까운 번역을 담았습니다.

이 책의 수준과 타깃 독자

- **미국 원어민 기준**: 유치원 ~ 초등학교 저학년
- **한국 학습자 기준**: 초등학교 저학년 ~ 중학생
- 영어원서 완독 경험이 없는 초보 영어 학습자 (토익 기준 450~750점대)
- **비슷한 수준의 다른 챕터북**: Arthur Chapter Book, Flat Stanley, Magic Tree House, Marvin Redpost
- **도서 분량**: 약 5,000단어

아이도 어른도 재미있게 읽는 영어 원서를
〈롱테일 에디션〉으로 만나 보세요!

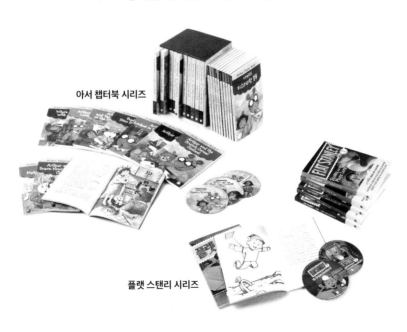

아서 챕터북 시리즈

플랫 스탠리 시리즈

Chapter 1

1. How did Spencer describe an astral body?

A. It protected a person from serious harm.

B. It controlled a person's movements.

C. It looked much different from a regular body.

D. It could leave a person's normal body.

2. According to Spencer, what was a benefit of out-of-body traveling?

A. It did not require a lot of focus.

B. It felt similar to flying in a plane.

C. It was a convenient way to get somewhere.

D. It could be done at any time of the day.

3. What did Zack's dad mention?

A. There was a mouse in the apartment.

B. There was no food in the fridge.

C. He had to go out for an hour.

D. Spencer had to go home soon.

4. What was one of the instructions in the book?

A. To play soft music in the background

B. To lie down and close one's eyes

C. To keep one's hands pressed together

D. To cover one's forehead with a cloth

5. What did Zack feel before he got out of his body?

A. He felt something light against his hand.

B. He felt something sharp in his belly button.

C. He felt like his leg was becoming frozen.

D. He felt like his eyes were burning.

Check Your Reading Speed

1분에 몇 단어를 읽는지 리딩 속도를 측정해보세요.

$$\frac{883 \text{ words}}{\text{reading time (\quad) sec}} \times 60 = (\qquad) \text{ WPM}$$

Build Your Vocabulary

sleep over idiom (남의 집에서) 자고 가다, 자고 오다
If someone, especially a child, sleeps over in a place such as a friend's home, they stay there for one night.

⋆ **weird** [wiərd] a. 기이한, 기묘한; 기괴한, 섬뜩한
If you describe something or someone as weird, you mean that they are strange.

⋆ **trash** [træʃ] v. 엉망으로 만들다, 부수다; (필요 없는 것을) 버리다; n. 쓰레기
If someone trashes a place or vehicle, they deliberately destroy it or make it very dirty.

⋆ **electric** [iléktrik] a. 전기의; 전기를 이용하는 (electric shock n. 감전, 전기 충격)
If you get an electric shock, you get a sudden painful feeling when you touch something which is connected to a supply of electricity.

⋆ **parallel** [pǽrəlèl] a. 아주 유사한; 평행한; n. ~와 아주 유사한 것; v. ~와 유사하다
Parallel events or situations happen at the same time as one another, or are similar to one another.

⋆ **universe** [jú:nəvə:rs] n. 우주; 은하계; (특정한 유형의) 경험 세계
A universe can be a world or an area of space that is different from the one we are in.

⋆ **medicine** [médisn] n. 약, 약물; 의학, 의술, 의료
Medicine is a substance that you drink or swallow in order to cure an illness.

* **cabinet** [kǽbənit] n. 캐비닛, 보관장; (정부의) 내각
A cabinet is a cupboard used for storing things such as medicine or alcoholic drinks or for displaying decorative things in.

* **stuff** [stʌf] n. 일, 것, 물건; v. 쑤셔 넣다; 채워 넣다
You can use stuff to refer to things such as a substance, a collection of things, events, or ideas, or the contents of something in a general way without mentioning the thing itself by name.

‡ **include** [inklú:d] v. 포함하다; ~을 (~에) 포함시키다
If one thing includes another thing, it has the other thing as one of its parts.

be up for idiom 기꺼이 ~하려고 하다
If you are up for something, you are willing to take part in a particular activity.

‡ **float** [flout] v. (물 위나 공중에서) 떠가다; (물에) 뜨다; n. 부표
Something that floats in or through the air hangs in it or moves slowly and gently through it.

‡ **exact** [igzǽkt] a. 정확한; 꼼꼼한, 빈틈없는 (exactly ad. 정확히)
You use exactly with a question to ask for more information about something.

‡ **regular** [régjulər] a. 보통의, 평상시의; 규칙적인, 정기적인 ; n. 단골손님
Regular is used to mean normal, ordinary, or usual.

‡ **lean** [li:n] v. ~에 기대다; 기울이다, (몸을) 숙이다; a. 군살이 없는, 호리호리한
If you lean on or against someone or something, you rest against them so that they partly support your weight.

brand-new [brǽnd-njú:] a. 아주 새로운, 신상품의
A brand-new object is completely new.

bunk [bʌŋk] n. (= bunk bed) 이층 침대; (배나 기차의) 침상
Bunk beds are two beds fixed one above the other in a frame.

backpack [bǽkpæk] n. 책가방, 배낭
A backpack is a bag with straps that go over your shoulders, so that you can carry things on your back when you are walking or climbing.

⁎ **journey** [dʒə́ːrni] n. (특히 멀리 가는) 여행, 여정; v. 여행하다
When you make a journey, you travel from one place to another.

⁑ **used** [juːzd] a. 헌 것의, 중고품의; ~에 익숙한 (used-book n. 중고책)
A used book is owned by someone else before you.

⁑ **load** [loud] n. (수·양이) 많음; (많은 양의) 짐; v. (짐·사람 등을) 싣다
If you refer to a load of people or things or loads of them, you are emphasizing that there are a lot of them.

⁎ **bet** [bet] v. (~이) 틀림없다; (내기 등에) 돈을 걸다; n. 짐작, 추측; 내기
You use expressions such as 'I bet,' 'I'll bet,' and 'you can bet' to indicate that you are sure something is true.

⁎ **metal** [metl] n. 금속; a. 금속제의
Metal is a hard substance such as iron, steel, gold, or lead.

⁎ **detect** [ditékt] v. 탐지하다; 발견하다; 찾아내다 (metal detector n. 금속 탐지기)
A metal detector is a piece of equipment used especially at airports for checking whether someone is carrying something such as a weapon.

⁎ **divorce** [divɔ́ːrs] v. 이혼하다; n. 이혼 (divorced a. 이혼한)
If two people divorce or if one of them divorces the other, their marriage is legally ended.

snack [snæk] n. 간식; v. 간식을 먹다
A snack is a small amount of food that you eat between meals.

⁑ **company** [kʌ́mpəni] n. 손님; 동료; 같이 있음; 회사
If you have company, you have a visitor or friend with you.

⁎ **pajamas** [pədʒáˑməz] n. (바지와 상의로 된) 잠옷
A pair of pajamas consists of comfortable pants and a shirt that you wear when you sleep.

sleepover [slí:pòuvər] n. 함께 자며 놀기
A sleepover is an occasion when someone, especially a child, sleeps for one night in a place such as a friend's home.

turn off idiom (전기·기계 등을) 끄다; (수도·가스 등을) 잠그다
When you turn off a piece of equipment such as a television or light, you stop it working temporarily by pressing a button or by moving a switch.

turn on idiom (전기·기계 등을) 켜다; (수도꼭지 등을) 틀다
When you turn on a piece of equipment such as a television or light, you make it start working by pressing a button or moving a switch.

★**flashlight** [flǽʃlait] n. 손전등; 회중 전등
A flashlight is a small electric light which gets its power from batteries and which you can carry in your hand.

get set idiom 준비를 갖추다
If you get set for something, you get yourself ready for it.

groovy [grú:vi] a. 멋진, 근사한
If you describe something as groovy, you mean that it is attractive, fashionable, or exciting.

★**chime** [ʧaim] n. 차임, 종; v. (종이나 시계가) 울리다
Chimes are a set of small objects which make a ringing sound when they are blown by the wind.

at one with idiom ~와 하나가 되어
If you are at one with something, you are in a peaceful state as a part of it.

★**forehead** [fɔ́:rhèd] n. 이마
Your forehead is the area at the front of your head between your eyebrows and your hair.

★**belly** [béli] n. 배, 복부 (belly button n. 배꼽)
Your belly button is the small round thing in the center of your stomach.

navel [néivəl] n. 배꼽
Your navel is the small hollow just below your waist at the front of your body.

* **superior** [səpíəriər] a. 거만한; 우월한; 뛰어난; 상급의; n. 상급자, 상관
If you describe someone as superior, you disapprove of them because they behave as if they are better, more important, or more intelligent than other people.

* **interpret** [intə́:rprit] v. 설명하다, 해석하다; 통역하다
If you interpret something, you explain the meaning of it.

seep [si:p] v. 스며 나오다, 새다; 침투하다
If something seeps out of somewhere, it moves or spreads slowly out of or through there.

* **shoot** [ʃu:t] v. (shot-shot) (눈길 등을) 휙 던지다; (총 등을) 쏘다; 휙 움직이다; n. 발사
If you shoot a look at someone, you look at them quickly and briefly, often in a way that expresses your feelings.

go on idiom 말을 계속하다; (어떤 상황이) 계속되다; (어떤 일을) 계속하다
To go on means to continue speaking after a short pause.

* **smoke** [smouk] n. 연기; v. (담배를) 피우다; 연기를 내뿜다
Smoke is a grey, black, or white cloud produced by something that is burning.

* **direction** [dirékʃən] n. (pl.) 지시; 방향; 위치
Directions are instructions that tell you what to do, how to do something, or how to get somewhere.

* **tickle** [tikl] n. 간지러움; (장난으로) 간지럽히기; v. 간지럽히다; 재미있게 하다
Tickle is a sensation of light stroking or itching.

stuck [stʌk] a. 움직일 수 없는, 꼼짝 못하는; 갇힌
If something is stuck in a particular position, it is fixed tightly in this position and is unable to move.

* **pop** [pap] v. 불쑥 나타나다; 펑 하는 소리가 나다; 눈이 휘둥그레지다; n. 펑 (하는 소리)
When something pops, it comes suddenly or unexpectedly out of or away from something else.

bob [bab] v. 위아래로 움직이다; (고개를) 까닥거리다; n. (머리·몸을) 까닥거림
If something bobs, it moves up and down, like something does when it is floating on water.

* **ceiling** [síːliŋ] n. 천장
A ceiling is the horizontal surface that forms the top part or roof inside a room.

Chapter 2

1. **What did the floating Spencer look like?**

   A. He looked much smaller than the real Spencer.

   B. His body looked somewhat thin.

   C. He looked kind of transparent.

   D. His skin looked really pale.

2. **Why did Zack enjoy being out of his body?**

   A. It was awesome to move in the air.

   B. It was exciting to watch his regular body.

   C. It was cool to walk on the ceiling.

   D. It was fun not needing to breathe.

3. Why was Spencer interested in going to Egypt?

   A. He had heard that the food there was delicious.

   B. He had always wanted to see a pyramid.

   C. He had not been there since he was little.

   D. He had studied it for school recently.

4. Why did Zack and Spencer decide to go to the Bronx Zoo?

   A. Zack knew his dad would not want him to go to Egypt.

   B. Zack wanted to return home before his dad saw he was gone.

   C. They thought seeing the animals at night would be entertaining.

   D. They liked the idea of sneaking in and playing with the animals.

5. What did Zack realize about out-of-body travel?

   A. It was not necessary to use his arms and legs at all.

   B. It was difficult to float in the right direction.

   C. It was not possible to open doors that were shut.

   D. It was easy to move walls with his hands.

Check Your Reading Speed

1분에 몇 단어를 읽는지 리딩 속도를 측정해보세요.

$$\frac{549 \text{ words}}{\text{reading time ( ) sec}} \times 60 = (\quad) \text{ WPM}$$

Build Your Vocabulary

★ **yell** [jel] v. 소리 지르다, 고함치다; n. 고함, 외침
If you yell, you shout loudly, often when you want to get someone's attention or because you are angry, excited, or in pain.

복습 **ceiling** [síːliŋ] n. 천장
A ceiling is the horizontal surface that forms the top part or roof inside a room.

★ **peer** [piər] v. 유심히 보다, 눈여겨보다; n. 또래
If you peer at something, you look at it very hard, usually because it is difficult to see clearly.

복습 **forehead** [fɔ́ːrhèd] n. 이마
Your forehead is the area at the front of your head between your eyebrows and your hair.

복습 **belly** [béli] n. 배, 복부 (belly button n. 배꼽)
Your belly button is the small round thing in the center of your stomach.

복습 **weird** [wiərd] a. 기이한, 기묘한; 기괴한, 섬뜩한
If you describe something or someone as weird, you mean that they are strange.

복습 **bunk** [bʌŋk] n. (배나 기차의) 침상; 이층 침대; v. 침대에서 자다
A bunk is one of two beds that attached together.

bob [bab] v. 위아래로 움직이다; (고개를) 까닥거리다; n. (머리·몸을) 까닥거림
If something bobs, it moves up and down, like something does when it is floating on water.

★**sparkle** [spaːrkl] v. 반짝이다; 생기 넘치다; n. 반짝거림, 광채 (sparkly a. 반짝반짝 빛나는)
Sparkly things are shining brightly with a lot of small points of light.

★**amaze** [əméiz] v. (대단히) 놀라게 하다 (amazing a. 놀라운)
You say that something is amazing when it is very surprising and makes you feel pleasure, approval, or wonder.

※**weight** [weit] n. 무게; 체중; 무거운 것
The weight of a person or thing is how heavy they are, measured in units such as kilograms, pounds, or tons.

※**breathe** [briːð] v. 숨을 쉬다, 호흡하다; 숨을 돌리다; 살아 있다
When people or animals breathe, they take air into their lungs and let it out again.

※**sink** [siŋk] v. 가라앉다, 빠지다; 박다; (구멍을) 파다; n. (부엌의) 개수대
If something sinks, it moves slowly downward.

※**grin** [grin] n. 활짝 웃음; v. 이를 드러내고 싱긋 웃다; (아파서) 이를 악물다
Grin is a big smile that shows your teeth.

※**geography** [dʒiágrəfi] n. 지리학; (한 지역의) 지리, 지형
Geography is the study of the countries of the world and of such things as the land, seas, climate, towns, and population.

★**cube** [kjuːb] n. 정육면체; v. (음식 재료를) 깍둑썰기하다 (sugar cube n. 각설탕)
A sugar cube is a small hard piece of sugar with six sides that you put in a hot drink.

※**otherwise** [ʌðərwàiz] ad. 그렇지 않으면; 그 외에는; 다른 방법으로
You use otherwise after stating a situation or fact, in order to say what the result or consequence would be if this situation or fact was not the case.

복습 float [flout] v. (물 위나 공중에서) 떠가다; (물에) 뜨다; n. 부표
Something that floats in or through the air hangs in it or moves slowly and gently through it.

⁎ grip [grip] v. 꽉 잡다, 움켜잡다; (마음·흥미·시선을) 끌다; n. 꽉 붙잡음, 통제
If you grip something, you take hold of it with your hand and continue to hold it firmly.

doorknob [dɔ́:rnàb] n. 문손잡이
A doorknob is a round handle on a door that you turn to open and close the door.

⁎ scissors [sízərz] n. 가위
Scissors are a small cutting tool with two sharp blades that are screwed together. You use scissors for cutting things such as paper and cloth.

⁎ dive [daiv] v. (dove-dived) 휙 움직이다; (물속으로) 뛰어들다; 급강하하다;
n. (물속으로) 뛰어들기
If you dive in a particular direction or into a particular place, you jump or move there quickly.

⁎ disappear [disəpíər] v. 사라지다, 보이지 않게 되다; 없어지다; 실종되다
If you say that someone or something disappears, you mean that you can no longer see them, usually because you or they have changed position.

⁎ slide [slaid] v. (slid-slid) 미끄러지듯이 움직이다; 슬며시 넣다; n. 떨어짐; 미끄러짐
When something slides somewhere or when you slide it there, it moves there smoothly over or against something.

awesome [ɔ́:səm] a. 기막히게 좋은, 굉장한; 어마어마한, 엄청난
When you describe something is awesome, you think it is extremely good.

⁎ flash [flæʃ] n. 섬광; 번쩍임; (감정·생각 등이) 갑자기 떠오름; v. 번쩍이다; 휙 움직이다
Flash is a bright light that appears for a very short time.

⁎ brick [brik] n. 벽돌
Bricks are rectangular blocks of baked clay used for building walls, which are usually red or brown.

yikes [jaiks] int. 이크, 으악 (놀랐을 때 내는 소리)
Yikes is used to show that you are worried, surprised, or shocked.

✽ **story** [stɔ́:ri] n. (= storey) 건물의 층; 이야기; 줄거리
A story of a building is one of its different levels, which is situated above or below other levels.

✱ **underneath** [ʌ̀ndərní:θ] prep. ~의 밑에, ~의 아래에
If one thing is underneath another, it is directly under it, and may be covered or hidden by it.

✽ **tiny** [táini] a. 아주 작은
Something or someone that is tiny is extremely small.

Chapter 3

1. What did Zack do before stopping at the zoo?

A. He acted like a flight attendant making an announcement.

B. He pretended to be a superhero fighting bad guys.

C. He gave Spencer a tour of the whole city.

D. He looked around places he had never seen before.

2. What did Zack and Spencer find when they arrived at the zoo?

A. All the visitors were about to leave.

B. The cages were empty and clean.

C. The zoo was dark and deserted.

D. The animals were wandering around.

3. Why did Zack think it would be safe to see the lions?

A. The lions would never attack humans.

B. The lions were trained to be nice.

C. Zack and Spencer would stand far away.

D. Zack and Spencer were not in their normal bodies.

4. What was true about the big lion?

A. He had not eaten anything all day.

B. He could feel Zack and Spencer's presence.

C. He saw Zack and Spencer in front of him.

D. He was terrified of astral bodies.

5. What did Zack try to do?

A. Dive through the lion to prove he was brave

B. Get the lion to copy his movements

C. Go around the lion to get out of the cave

D. Make loud sounds to scare the lion

Check Your Reading Speed

1분에 몇 단어를 읽는지 리딩 속도를 측정해보세요.

$$\frac{682 \text{ words}}{\text{reading time ( ) sec}} \times 60 = (\quad) \text{ wPM}$$

Build Your Vocabulary

★ **panic** [pǽnik] v. (panicked-panicked) 어쩔 줄 모르다; n. 극심한 공포; 허둥지둥함
If you panic, you suddenly feel anxious or afraid, and act quickly and without thinking carefully.

☆ **rush** [rʌʃ] v. 급히 움직이다; 달려들다; n. 돌진; 혼잡; (감정이 갑자기) 치밀어 오름
If water, another liquid or air rushes somewhere, it moves quickly.

☆ **lung** [lʌŋ] n. 폐, 허파
Your lungs are the two organs inside your chest which fill with air when you breathe in.

복습 **breathe** [briːð] v. 숨을 쉬다, 호흡하다; 숨을 돌리다; 살아 있다
When people or animals breathe, they take air into their lungs and let it out again.

★ **giggle** [gigl] v. 킥킥거리다; 낄낄 웃다; n. 킥킥거림; 피식 웃음
If someone giggles, they laugh in a childlike way, because they are amused, nervous, or embarrassed.

uptown [ʌptáun] ad. 도심을 벗어나; 시 외곽으로; a. 시 외곽의
If you go uptown, or go to a place uptown, you go away from the center of a town or city toward the edge.

☆ **captain** [kǽptən] n. (항공기의) 기장; 선장; (스포츠 팀의) 주장; v. (운동 팀의) 주장이 되다
The captain of an airplane is the pilot in charge of it.

be about to idiom 막 ~하려는 참이다
If you are about to do something, you are going to do it immediately.

land [lænd] v. (땅·표면에) 내려앉다, 착륙하다; 놓다, 두다; n. 육지, 땅; 지역
When someone lands a plane, ship, or spacecraft, or when it lands, it arrives somewhere after a journey.

secure [sikjúər] a. 단단한; 안전한; 안심하는; v. (단단히) 고정시키다; 얻어 내다
(securely ad. 단단히)
If an object is secure, it is fixed firmly in position.

fasten [fæsn] v. 매다, 채우다; 고정시키다; (단단히) 잠그다
When you fasten something, you close it by means of buttons or a strap, or some other device.

tray [trei] n. 쟁반 (tray table n. 쟁반 같은 탁자)
A tray table is a small table that folds down from the back of the seat in front of you in a plane or train.

upright [ʌ́prait] a. 수직으로 세워 둔; (자세가) 똑바른
Something that is upright stands straight up.

lock [lak] v. 고정시키다; (자물쇠로) 잠그다; n. 잠금장치
If you lock something in a particular position or if it locks there, it is held or fitted firmly in that position.

go on idiom 말을 계속하다; (어떤 상황이) 계속되다; (어떤 일을) 계속하다
To go on means to continue speaking after a short pause.

pleasant [plézənt] a. 쾌적한, 즐거운; 상냥한
Something that is pleasant is nice, enjoyable, or attractive.

frequent [frí:kwənt] a. 자주 ~하는; 빈번한; 상습적인; v. 자주 가다
If something is frequent, it happens often.

flight [flait] n. 비행기 여행; 항공편; 계단; 탈출
A flight is a journey made by flying, usually in an airplane.

* worth [wəːrθ] a. ~의 가치가 있는; ~해 볼 만한; n. 가치, 값어치
If something is worth a particular value, it has that value, especially in money.

* except [iksépt] prep. (= except for) ~를 제외하고, ~외에는; v. 제외하다
You use except for to introduce the only thing or person that prevents a statement from being completely true.

come to think of it idiom 그러고 보니, 생각해 보니
You use 'come to think of it,' when you mention something that you have suddenly remembered or realized.

* count [kaunt] v. 간주되다, 여겨지다; (수를) 세다; 계산하다; n. 셈, 계산; 수치
If something counts or is counted as a particular thing, it is regarded as being that thing, especially in particular circumstances or under particular rules.

★ howl [haul] v. (개·늑대 등이) 울부짖다; 아우성치다; n. (개·늑대 등의) 길게 짖는 소리
If an animal such as a wolf or a dog howls, it makes a long, loud, crying sound.

creepy [kríːpi] a. 오싹하게 하는, 으스스한; (섬뜩할 정도로) 기이한
If you say that something or someone is creepy, you mean they make you feel very nervous or frightened.

* nod [nad] v. (고개를) 끄덕이다, 까딱하다; n. (고개를) 끄덕임
If you nod, you move your head downward and upward to show that you are answering 'yes' to a question, or to show agreement, understanding, or approval.

be crazy about idiom ~에 미치다, 열광하다
If you are crazy about something, you are very enthusiastic about it.

복습 bet [bet] v. (~이) 틀림없다; (내기 등에) 돈을 걸다; n. 짐작, 추측; 내기
You use expressions such as 'I bet,' 'I'll bet,' and 'you can bet' to indicate that you are sure something is true.

★ **cave** [keiv] n. 동굴
A cave is a large hole in the side of a cliff or hill, or one that is under the ground.

out of one's mind idiom 제정신이 아닌
If you say that someone is out of their mind, you mean that they are mad or very foolish.

★ **logic** [ládʒik] n. 타당성; 논리; 논리학
The logic of a conclusion or an argument is its quality of being correct and reasonable.

★ **snore** [snɔːr] v. 코를 골다; n. 코 고는 소리
When someone who is asleep snores, they make a loud noise each time they breathe.

★ **bunch** [bʌnʧ] n. (양·수가) 많음; 송이, 묶음; v. 단단해지다
A bunch of something is a large number or amount of it.

⚹ **huge** [hjuːdʒ] a. 거대한, 막대한
Something or someone that is huge is extremely large in size.

pussycat [púsikæt] n. 야옹이; 고양이
Children often refer to a cat as a pussycat.

⚹ **cough** [kɔːf] v. 기침하다; (기침을 하여 무엇을) 토하다; n. 기침
When you cough, you force air out of your throat with a sudden, harsh noise, especially when you have a cold.

★ **roar** [rɔːr] n. 으르렁거리는 소리; 함성; 굉음; v. 으르렁거리다; 고함치다
A roar is the loud deep sound that a lion makes.

★ **whisper** [hwíspər] v. 속삭이다, 귓속말을 하다; n. 속삭임, 소곤거리는 소리
When you whisper, you say something very quietly, using your breath rather than your throat, so that only one person can hear you.

★ **dumb** [dʌm] a. 멍청한, 바보 같은; 말을 못 하는
If you say that something is dumb, you think that it is silly and annoying.

* bite [bait] v. (이빨로) 물다; (곤충·뱀 등이) 물다; n. 물기; 한 입; 소량의 음식
If an animal or person bites you, they use their teeth to hurt or injure you.

butt [bʌt] n. 엉덩이; 남은 토막; v. (머리로) 들이받다
Someone's butt is the part of their body that they sit on.

have got a point idiom 일리가 있다
If you say that someone has got a point, you mean that you accept that what they have said is important and should be considered.

* entrance [éntrəns] n. 입구, 문; 입장, 등장
Entrance is the place where you can enter a room, building, or an area.

used [juːzd] a. ~에 익숙한; 헌 것의, 중고품의 (get used to idiom ~에 익숙해지다)
If you get used to something or someone, you become familiar with it or get to know them, so that you no longer feel that the thing or person is unusual or surprising.

* wave [weiv] v. (손·팔을) 흔들다; 흔들리다; n. 물결; (팔·손·몸을) 흔들기
If you wave or wave your hand, you move your hand from side to side in the air, to say hello or goodbye or as a signal.

** notice [nóutis] v. 알아채다, 인지하다; 주의하다; n. 신경 씀, 주목, 알아챔
If you notice something or someone, you become aware of them.

* yawn [jɔːn] v. 하품하다; n. 하품
If you yawn, you open your mouth very wide and breathe in more air than usual, often when you are tired or bored.

** sense [sens] v. 감지하다; (기계가) 탐지하다; n. 감각; 느낌; 인지
If you sense something, you become aware of it or you realize it, although it is not very obvious.

dive [daiv] v. (dove-dived) 휙 움직이다; (물속으로) 뛰어들다; 급강하하다;
n. (물속으로) 뛰어들기
If you dive in a particular direction or into a particular place, you jump or move there quickly.

Chapter 4

1. **What did Zack and Spencer do at the amusement park?**

   A. They went on every single ride together.

   B. They used themselves as roller coasters.

   C. They went up and down the hills in cars.

   D. They turned on the lights to all the rides.

2. **Why was there a long line near Times Square?**

   A. People were waiting to check out a new store.

   B. People were waiting to buy a new video game.

   C. People were waiting to watch a new movie.

   D. People were waiting to see a new play.

3. **What did Zack discover when he went inside?**

    A. He could not eat the snack that he wanted.

    B. He forgot to bring money to buy things.

    C. He did not have enough time to play games.

    D. He was uncomfortable being around so many people.

4. **Why did Zack want to go home?**

    A. He missed being in his normal body.

    B. He did not like being invisible to everyone.

    C. He was so bored that he was about to fall asleep.

    D. He did not want to watch something so scary.

5. **What did Spencer think about going home?**

    A. He agreed that he and Zack needed sleep.

    B. He thought that an astral body did not need sleep.

    C. He assumed that it would take a while to get home.

    D. He felt like anything would be better than going home.

Check Your Reading Speed

1분에 몇 단어를 읽는지 리딩 속도를 측정해보세요.

$$\frac{472 \text{ words}}{\text{reading time ( ) sec}} \times 60 = (\quad) \text{ wPM}$$

Build Your Vocabulary

slide [slaid] v. (slid-slid) 미끄러지듯이 움직이다; 슬며시 넣다; n. 떨어짐; 미끄러짐
When something slides somewhere or when you slide it there, it moves there smoothly over or against something.

zoom [zu:m] v. 쌩 하고 가다; 급증하다; n. 쌩 하고 지나가는 소리
If you zoom somewhere, you go there very quickly.

amusement park [əmjú:zmənt pa:rk] n. 놀이공원
An amusement park is a large park that has a lot of things that you can ride and play on and many different activities to enjoy.

desert [dizə́:rt] ① v. 떠나다; 버리다 (deserted a. 사람이 없는; 버림받은) ② n. 사막
A deserted place has no people in it.

hump [hʌmp] n. 툭 솟아 오른 곳; (낙타 등의) 혹
A hump is a small hill or raised area.

dinosaur [dáinəsɔ̀:r] n. 공룡
Dinosaurs were large reptiles which lived in prehistoric times.

skeleton [skélətn] n. 뼈대; 골격; 해골; (건물 등의) 뼈대
Skeleton is the set of bones that supports a human or animal body, or a model of this.

weird [wiərd] a. 기이한, 기묘한; 기괴한, 섬뜩한
If you describe something or someone as weird, you mean that they are strange.

headfirst [hedfə́:rst] ad. 거꾸로, 곤두박질로; 몹시 서둘러서, 황급히
If you move headfirst in a particular direction, you move with your head in front of the rest of your body while you move forward.

‡suggest [səgdʒést] v. 추천하다; (아이디어·계획을) 제안하다; 시사하다
If you suggest something, you offer an idea or a plan for someone to consider.

＊statue [stǽtʃuː] n. 조각상
A statue is a large sculpture of a person or an animal, made of stone or metal.

‡liberty [líbərti] n. 자유; 해방; 권리
Liberty is the freedom to live your life in the way that you want, without interference from other people or the authorities.

＊torch [tɔːrtʃ] n. 횃불; 손전등
A torch is a long stick with burning material at one end, used to provide light or to set things on fire.

awesome [ɔ́ːsəm] a. 기막히게 좋은, 굉장한; 어마어마한, 엄청난
When you describe something is awesome, you think it is extremely good.

yell [jel] v. 소리 지르다, 고함치다; n. 고함, 외침
If you yell, you shout loudly, often when you want to get someone's attention or because you are angry, excited, or in pain.

booger [búgər] n. 코딱지; 눈곱; 도깨비
A booger is a piece of the dried substance from inside your nose.

uptown [ʌptáun] ad. 도심을 벗어나; 시 외곽으로; a. 시 외곽의
If you go uptown, or go to a place uptown, you go away from the center of a town or city toward the edge.

‡stretch [stretʃ] v. 뻗어 있다, 펼쳐지다; 늘이다; n. 기지개 켜기
Something that stretches over an area or distance covers or exists in the whole of that area or distance.

‡ block [blak] n. (도로로 나뉘는) 구역, 블록; 사각형 덩어리; v. 막다, 차단하다
A block in a town is an area of land with streets on all its sides.

‡ million [míljən] n. 100만; 수많은
A million or one million is the number 1,000,000.

‡ horrible [hɔ́ːrəbl] a. 소름끼치는, 무시무시한; 못된; 지긋지긋한
You can call something horrible when it causes you to feel great shock, fear, and disgust.

help oneself to idiom (음식 등을) 마음대로 집어먹다, 자유로이 먹다
If you help yourself to something, you serve yourself or you take it for yourself.

‡ hit [hit] v. (hit-hit) (생각 등이 불현듯) 떠오르다; 부딪치다; 치다; n. 치기
When a feeling or an idea hits you, it suddenly affects you or comes into your mind.

bummer [bʌ́mər] n. 실망스러운 일; 불쾌한 경험
If you say that something is a bummer, you mean that it is unpleasant or disappointing.

‡ bunch [bʌntʃ] n. (양·수가) 많음; 송이, 묶음; v. 단단해지다
A bunch of something is a large number or amount of it.

★ lobby [lábi] n. 로비(공공 건물의 현관); (정치적인) 로비
Lobby is the area just inside the entrance to a hotel, theater, or other large building.

‡ control [kəntróul] n. (기계·차량의) 제어 장치; 통제, 제어; v. 지배하다; 조정하다
A control is a device such as a switch or lever which you use in order to operate a machine or other piece of equipment.

★ slip [slip] v. 빠져나가다; 미끄러지다; 슬며시 가다; n. 미끄러짐; 실수; 작은 조각
If something slips, it slides out of place or out of your hand.

‡ stuck [stʌk] a. 갇힌; 움직일 수 없는, 꼼짝 못하는
If you are stuck in a boring or unpleasant situation, you are unable to change it or get away from it.

ceiling [síːliŋ] n. 천장
A ceiling is the horizontal surface that forms the top part or roof inside a room.

scary [skέəri] a. 무서운, 겁나는
Something that is scary is rather frightening.

★**mess** [mes] n. (지저분하고) 엉망인 상태; (많은 문제로) 엉망인 상황; v. 엉망으로 만들다
If someone is a mess, they look dirty and untidy, or are in a bad emotional state.

asleep [əslíːp] a. 잠이 든
Someone who is asleep is sleeping.

stay out idiom (밤에) 집에 안 들어오다, 외박하다
If you stay out at night, you remain away from home, especially when you are expected to be there.

★**adventure** [ædvénʧər] n. 모험; 모험심
If someone has an adventure, they become involved in an unusual, exciting, and rather dangerous journey or series of events.

Chapter 5

1. **What were Zack and Spencer going to do with the book?**
   A. Find out how to wake up their sleeping bodies
   B. Find out how to re-enter their real bodies
   C. Find out how to fall asleep in their astral bodies
   D. Find out how to move things with their astral bodies

2. **What problem did Zack and Spencer have with the book?**
   A. The book was too heavy for them to lift.
   B. The page they needed had been removed.
   C. The directions contained too many steps for them to follow.
   D. The instructions were on a page that they could not see.

3. What did Zack attempt to do to wake up his dad?

A. Push him off the bed

B. Shout at him

C. Take away his pillow

D. Open his eyes

4. Why did Spencer suggest going to Mrs. Coleman-Levin's house?

A. She might have an idea of how to help.

B. She could recommend another book to use.

C. She was an expert at solving problems.

D. She stayed up all night doing science research.

5. What did Zack and Spencer see in Mrs. Coleman-Levin's apartment?

A. They saw several pets running around.

B. They saw ordinary plants arranged beautifully.

C. They saw that Mrs. Coleman-Levin's normal body was asleep.

D. They saw that Mrs. Coleman-Levin's astral body was doing chores.

Check Your Reading Speed

1분에 몇 단어를 읽는지 리딩 속도를 측정해보세요.

$$\frac{590 \text{ words}}{\text{reading time ( ) sec}} \times 60 = (\quad) \text{ wPM}$$

Build Your Vocabulary

^{복습}**slide** [slaid] v. (slid-slid) 미끄러지듯이 움직이다; 슬며시 넣다; n. 떨어짐; 미끄러짐
When something slides somewhere or when you slide it there, it moves there smoothly over or against something.

^{복습}**weird** [wiərd] a. 기이한, 기묘한; 기괴한, 섬뜩한
If you describe something or someone as weird, you mean that they are strange.

^{복습}**float** [flout] v. (물 위나 공중에서) 떠가다; (물에) 뜨다; n. 부표
Something that floats in or through the air hangs in it or moves slowly and gently through it.

^{복습}**bunk** [bʌŋk] n. (배나 기차의) 침상; 이층 침대; v. 침대에서 자다
A bunk is one of two beds that attached together.

^{복습}**direction** [dirékʃən] n. (pl.) 지시; 방향; 위치
Directions are instructions that tell you what to do, how to do something, or how to get somewhere.

★**smack** [smæk] v. 탁 소리가 나게 치다; 세게 부딪치다; n. 찰싹 때리기; 탁 (하는 소리)
If you smack someone, you hit them with your hand.

^{복습}**forehead** [fɔ́:rhèd] n. 이마
Your forehead is the area at the front of your head between your eyebrows and your hair.

★**shrug** [ʃrʌg] v. (어깨를) 으쓱하다; n. 어깨를 으쓱하기
If you shrug, you move your shoulders up and let them drop to show that you do not know something or do not care.

‡**nervous** [nɔ́:rvəs] a. 초조해하는, 불안해하는 (nervously ad. 초조하게)
If someone is nervous, they are frightened or worried about something.

spook [spu:k] v. 겁먹게 하다; 겁먹다; n. 유령, 귀신
If something spooks you, it makes you suddenly feel frightened or nervous.

복습**asleep** [əslí:p] a. 잠이 든 (fast asleep idiom 깊이 잠든)
Someone who is fast asleep is sleeping deeply.

drool [dru:l] v. 침을 흘리다; (탐이 나서) 군침을 흘리다; n. 침
If a person or animal drools, saliva drops slowly from their mouth.

★**pillow** [pílou] n. 베개
A pillow is a rectangular cushion which you rest your head on when you are in bed.

복습**yell** [jel] v. 소리 지르다, 고함치다; n. 고함, 외침
If you yell, you shout loudly, often when you want to get someone's attention or because you are angry, excited, or in pain.

복습**go on** idiom (어떤 일을) 계속하다; (어떤 상황이) 계속되다; 말을 계속하다
If you go on doing something, or go on with an activity, you continue to do it.

‡**lip** [lip] n. 입술; 가장자리
Your lips are the two outer parts of the edge of your mouth.

★**sound** [saund] a. (잠이) 깊은; 믿을 만한; n. 소리; v. ~처럼 들리다
If someone is in a sound sleep, they are sleeping very deeply.

‡**inch** [inʧ] n. 조금, 약간; v. 조금씩 움직이다
An inch can refer to a very small distance or amount.

homeroom [hóumrum] n. 생활 학급
In a school, homeroom is the class or room where students in the same grade meet to get general information and be checked for attendance.

⚹ **brain** [brein] n. 뇌
Your brain is the organ inside your head that controls your body's activities and enables you to think and to feel things such as heat and pain.

⚹ **jar** [dʒɑːr] n. (잼·꿀 등을 담아 두는) 병; 단지; 항아리
A jar is a glass container with a lid that is used for storing food.

⚹ **boot** [buːt] n. 목이 긴 신발, 부츠 (work boot n. 작업용 부츠)
Boots are shoes that cover your whole foot and the lower part of your leg.

dressy [drési] a. 정장을 입어야 하는; 옷차림에 신경 쓰는; 멋진
A dressy occasion is one at which people wear very formal clothes.

morgue [mɔːrg] n. 시체 안치소, 영안실
A morgue is a building or a room where dead bodies are kept before they are buried or burned, or before they are identified or examined.

복습 **stuff** [stʌf] n. 일, 것, 물건; v. 쑤셔 넣다; 채워 넣다
You can use stuff to refer to things such as a substance, a collection of things, events, or ideas, or the contents of something in a general way without mentioning the thing itself by name.

stay up idiom (늦게까지) 안 자다, 깨어 있다
If you stay up, you remain out of bed at a time when most people have gone to bed or at a time when you are normally in bed yourself.

⚹ **dawn** [dɔːn] n. 새벽, 여명; v. 날이 새다; 이해되기 시작하다
Dawn is the time of day when light first appears in the sky, just before the sun rises.

⚹ **extra** [ékstrə] a. 추가의; 여분의; 특별한; 별도 계산의
You use extra to describe an amount, person, or thing that is added to others of the same kind, or that can be added to others of the same kind.

⚡ credit [krédit] n. 학점; 신용 거래; 칭찬; v. 믿다, 신용하다
Your credit in schoolwork is the mark you get, which indicates your level of achievement.

⚡ insect [ínsekt] n. 곤충
An insect is a small animal such as fly or ant, which has six legs, and sometimes wings.

⚡ feed [fiːd] v. 먹이를 주다; 먹여 살리다; 공급하다; n. (동물의) 먹이
If you feed a person or animal, you give them food to eat and sometimes actually put it in their mouths.

복습 huge [hjuːdʒ] a. 거대한, 막대한
Something or someone that is huge is extremely large in size.

★ tropical [trápikəl] a. 열대의, 열대 지방의
If you describe something as tropical, you mean that it is coming from or existing in the hottest parts of the world.

★ vine [vain] n. 덩굴 식물; 포도나무
A vine is a plant that grows up or over things, especially one which produces grapes.

★ waterfall [wɔ́ːtərfɔːl] n. 폭포
A waterfall is a place where water flows over the edge of a steep, high cliff in hills or mountains, and falls into a pool below.

cross-legged [krɔːs-légd] ad. 책상다리를 하고, 다리를 포개고
If someone is sitting cross-legged, they are sitting on the floor with their legs bent so that their knees point outward.

복습 ceiling [síːliŋ] n. 천장
A ceiling is the horizontal surface that forms the top part or roof inside a room.

Chapter
6

1. What was NOT true about Zack and Spencer?

A. They told Mrs. Coleman-Levin how they became astral bodies.

B. They listed places that they visited as astral bodies.

C. They found out how Mrs. Coleman-Levin got out of her body.

D. They were surprised that Mrs. Coleman-Levin was out of her body.

2. Why wouldn't Mrs. Coleman-Levin tell the boys how to get back into their bodies?

A. She was not sure how they could re-enter their bodies.

B. She felt like they should be punished for not being responsible.

C. She thought they should have more adventures in their astral bodies.

D. She wanted them to find a solution on their own.

3. What was Mrs. Coleman-Levin's advice?

A. To try some experiments

B. To ask someone else for help

C. To accept the truth and give up

D. To think about what they had learned in class

4. What did Mrs. Coleman-Levin say about astral bodies?

A. They understood things faster than people in normal bodies.

B. They could not be heard by people in normal bodies.

C. They were almost the same as normal bodies.

D. They were not as quick as normal bodies.

5. What would happen if Zack and Spencer did not re-enter their bodies soon?

A. Their real bodies would disappear from their homes.

B. Their families would have to figure out a way to save them.

C. They would remain astral bodies forever.

D. They would be considered absent from school.

Check Your Reading Speed
1분에 몇 단어를 읽는지 리딩 속도를 측정해보세요.

$$\frac{290 \text{ words}}{\text{reading time (} \quad \text{) sec}} \times 60 = (\quad\quad) \text{ wPM}$$

Build Your Vocabulary

★ **splendid** [spléndid] a. 정말 좋은, 훌륭한; 아주 인상적인
If you say that something is splendid, you mean that it is very good.

★★ **observe** [əbzə́ːrv] v. 관찰하다, 관측하다; (의견을) 말하다 (observation n. 관찰)
An observation is something that you have learned by seeing or watching something and thinking about it.

복습 **statue** [stǽʧuː] n. 조각상
A statue is a large sculpture of a person or an animal, made of stone or metal.

복습 **liberty** [líbərti] n. 자유; 해방; 권리
Liberty is the freedom to live your life in the way that you want, without interference from other people or the authorities.

figure out idiom ~을 이해하다, 알아내다; 계산하다, 산출하다
If you figure something out, you understand it or find the answer to it by thinking about it.

복습 **suggest** [səgdʒést] v. (아이디어·계획을) 제안하다; 추천하다; 시사하다
If you suggest something, you offer an idea or a plan for someone to consider.

★★ **experiment** [ikspérəmənt] v. 실험하다; n. 실험; 시험적인 행동
To experiment means to try out a new idea or method to see what it is like and what effects it has.

be big on idom ~을 대단히 좋아하다, ~에 열광하다
If you are big on something, you are very interested in it or enjoy it a lot.

bet [bet] v. (~이) 틀림없다; (내기 등에) 돈을 걸다; n. 짐작, 추측; 내기
You use expressions such as 'I bet,' 'I'll bet,' and 'you can bet' to indicate that you are sure something is true.

come up with idiom 생각해 내다; 찾아내다; 답을 제시하다
If you come up with something such as an idea, an answer to a question, or a solution to a problem, you think of it or suggest it.

＊**solution** [səlúːʃən] n. (문제·곤경의) 해법, 해결책
A solution to a problem or difficult situation is a way of dealing with it so that the difficulty is removed.

wave [weiv] v. (손·팔을) 흔들다; 흔들리다; n. 물결; (팔·손·몸을) 흔들기
If you wave or wave your hand, you move your hand from side to side in the air, to say hello or goodbye or as a signal.

be supposed to idiom ~해야 한다, ~하기로 되어 있다
If you are supposed to do something, you are expected to behave in a particular way, especially according to a rule, an agreement, or someone in authority.

＊**prompt** [prampt] a. 시간을 엄수하는; 즉각적인; v. (어떤 일이 일어나도록) 하다
(promptly ad. 정확히 제 시간에; 지체 없이)
If you do something promptly at a particular time, you do it at exactly that time.

＊**mark** [maːrk] v. 표시하다; 자국을 내다; 채점하다; n. 자국, 흔적; 표시
If you mark something with a particular word or symbol, you write that word or symbol on it.

＊**absent** [ǽbsənt] a. 결석한; 불참한; 없는; 멍한; v. 결석하다, 불참하다
(mark absent idiom 결석으로 표시하다)
If someone is absent, they are not in the place where they are expected to be, especially at school or work.

Chapter 7

1. What did Spencer do as part of the Scientific Method?

  A. He created a theory on how to solve their problem.

  B. He discussed all the ways they could reach their goal.

  C. He carefully observed every action the mouse took.

  D. He tested their belief that mice have good listening skills.

2. What was Zack and Spencer's plan for the mouse?

  A. They planned to teach him how to read directions.

  B. They planned to make him go onto the book.

  C. They planned to get him to move their real bodies.

  D. They planned to chase him out of the room.

3. **What did Zack's dad assume about the boys?**

   A. They were ignoring him.

   B. They were still out exploring.

   C. They had gone to bed very late.

   D. They had really left their bodies.

4. **How did Zack and Spencer find out the directions?**

   A. The book unexpectedly turned to the right page.

   B. They randomly guessed the correct thing to do.

   C. Zack's dad accidentally read the directions aloud.

   D. The mouse unknowingly tore the information out.

5. **What did Zack and Spencer have to do to re-enter their bodies?**

   A. Listen to the sound of their breath

   B. Put their astral hands inside their belly button

   C. Imagine they were waking up

   D. Lie in the same position as their real body

Check Your Reading Speed

1분에 몇 단어를 읽는지 리딩 속도를 측정해보세요.

$$\frac{1,619 \text{ words}}{\text{reading time ( ) sec}} \times 60 = (\quad) \text{ WPM}$$

Build Your Vocabulary

⋆ **scratch** [skrætʃ] v. (가려운 곳을) 긁다; 긁힌 자국을 내다; n. 긁힌 자국; 긁는 소리
If you scratch yourself, you rub your fingernails against your skin because it is itching.

snuggle [snʌgl] v. 바싹 파고들다; 달라붙다; 끌어안다
If you snuggle somewhere, you settle yourself into a warm, comfortable position, especially by moving closer to another person.

복습 **stuff** [stʌf] n. 일, 것, 물건; v. 쑤셔 넣다; 채워 넣다
You can use stuff to refer to things such as a substance, a collection of things, events, or ideas, or the contents of something in a general way without mentioning the thing itself by name.

복습 **bunk** [bʌŋk] n. (배나 기차의) 침상; 이층 침대; v. 침대에서 자다
A bunk is one of two beds that attached together.

복습 **float** [flout] v. (물 위나 공중에서) 떠가다; (물에) 뜨다; n. 부표
Something that floats in or through the air hangs in it or moves slowly and gently through it.

⋆ **unusual** [ʌnjúːʒuəl] a. 흔치 않은, 특이한, 드문
If something is unusual, it does not happen very often or you do not see it or hear it very often.

⋆ **glare** [glɛər] v. 노려보다; 환하다, 눈부시다; n. 노려봄; 환한 빛, 눈부심
If you glare at someone, you look at them with an angry expression on your face.

** fit [fit] v. 끼우다, 맞추다; (어떤 사람·사물에) 맞다; 적절하다; a. 적합한; 건강한
If you fit something into a particular space or place, you put it there.

nostril [nástrəl] n. 콧구멍
Your nostrils are the two openings at the end of your nose.

* punch [pʌntʃ] n. 주먹으로 한 대 침; v. 주먹으로 치다; 구멍을 뚫다
A punch is the action of hitting someone or something with your fist.

furry [fə́:ri] a. 털로 덮인; 털 같은
A furry animal is covered with thick, soft hair.

scamper [skǽmpər] v. 날쌔게 움직이다; 급히 사라지다
When people or small animals scamper somewhere, they move there quickly with small, light steps.

yikes [jaiks] int. 이크, 으악 (놀랐을 때 내는 소리)
Yikes is used to show that you are worried, surprised, or shocked.

dive [daiv] v. (dove-dived) 휙 움직이다; (물속으로) 뛰어들다; 급강하하다;
n. (물속으로) 뛰어들기
If you dive in a particular direction or into a particular place, you jump or move there quickly.

figure out idiom ~을 이해하다, 알아내다; 계산하다, 산출하다
If you figure something out, you understand it or find the answer to it by thinking about it.

mark [ma:rk] v. 표시하다; 자국을 내다; 채점하다; n. 자국, 흔적; 표시
If you mark something with a particular word or symbol, you write that word or symbol on it.

absent [ǽbsənt] a. 결석한; 불참한; 없는; 멍한; v. 결석하다, 불참하다
(mark absent idiom 결석으로 표시하다)
If someone is absent, they are not in the place where they are expected to be, especially at school or work.

never mind idiom ~은 신경 쓰지 마

You say never mind when you are emphasizing that something is not serious or important, often because something else is more important.

★**unconscious** [ʌnkánʃəs] a. 의식을 잃은, 의식이 없는; 무의식적인

Someone who is unconscious is in a state similar to sleep, usually as the result of a serious injury or a lack of oxygen.

복습**nod** [nad] v. (고개를) 끄덕이다, 까딱하다; n. (고개를) 끄덕임

If you nod, you move your head downward and upward to show that you are answering 'yes' to a question, or to show agreement, understanding, or approval.

★**react** [riǽkt] v. 반응을 보이다; 반항하다; 화학 반응을 일으키다

When you react to something that has happened to you, you behave in a particular way because of it.

★**genius** [dʒíːnjəs] n. 천재; 천재성; 특별한 재능

A genius is a highly talented, creative, or intelligent person.

‡**scientific** [sàiəntífik] a. 과학적인, 체계적인; 과학의

If you do something in a scientific way, you do it carefully and thoroughly, using experiments or tests.

‡**method** [méθəd] n. 방법, 방식

A method is a particular way of doing something.

복습**suggest** [səgdʒést] v. (아이디어·계획을) 제안하다; 추천하다; 시사하다

If you suggest something, you offer an idea or a plan for someone to consider.

‡**scientist** [sáiəntist] n. 과학자

A scientist is someone who has studied science and whose job is to teach or do research in science.

‡**solve** [salv] v. (문제·곤경을) 해결하다; (수학 문제 등을) 풀다

If you solve a problem or a question, you find a solution or an answer to it.

might as well idiom ~하는 게 좋겠다

If you say that you might as well do something, you do it because it seems best in the situation that you are in, although you may not really want to do it.

observe [əbzə́:rv] v. 관찰하다, 관측하다; (의견을) 말하다

If you observe a person or thing, you watch them carefully, especially in order to learn something about them.

form [fɔːrm] v. 형성하다; 기능을 하다; n. 종류, 유형; 방식

If you form a relationship, a habit, or an idea, or if it forms, it begins to exist and develop.

theory [θíːəri] n. (개인적인) 의견; 이론; 학설

If you have a theory about something, you have your own opinion about it which you cannot prove but which you think is true.

go on idiom 말을 계속하다; (어떤 상황이) 계속되다; (어떤 일을) 계속하다

To go on means to continue speaking after a short pause.

exact [igzǽkt] a. 정확한; 꼼꼼한, 빈틈없는 (exactly ad. 정확히)

You use exactly with a question to ask for more information about something.

have in mind idiom ~을 염두에 두다, 생각하다

If you ask someone what they have in mind, you want to know in more detail about an idea or wish they have.

rug [rʌg] n. (작은 카펫같이 생긴) 러그, 깔개

A rug is a piece of thick material that you put on a floor. It is like a carpet but covers a smaller area.

doubtful [dáutfəl] a. 확신이 없는, 의심을 품은; 불확실한

If you are doubtful about something, you feel unsure or uncertain about it.

sense [sens] v. 감지하다; (기계가) 탐지하다; n. 감각; 느낌; 인지

If you sense something, you become aware of it or you realize it, although it is not very obvious.

⁑ corner [kɔ́ːrnər] v. (구석에) 가두다, (궁지에) 몰아넣다; n. 모퉁이; 구석

If you corner a person or animal, you force them into a place they cannot escape from.

long shot [lɔ́ːŋ ʃat] n. 성공 확률이 낮은 것, 대담한 시도

If you describe something as a long shot, you mean that it is unlikely to succeed, but is worth trying.

go for idiom ~을 해 보다, 시도하다; ~을 좋아하다

If you go for something, you try to have or achieve it.

nibble [nibl] v. 갉아먹다; 조금씩 물어뜯다; n. 조금씩 물어뜯기, 한 입 분량

When an animal nibbles something, it takes small bites of it quickly and repeatedly.

⁑ favor [féivər] n. 친절한 행위; 부탁; 찬성; 인기; v. 편들다; 선호하다

If you do someone a favor, you do something for them even though you do not have to.

⁑ confuse [kənfjúːz] v. (사람을) 혼란시키다; 혼동하다; 어리둥절하게 하다
(confused a. 혼란스러워하는)

If you are confused, you do not know exactly what is happening or what to do.

복습 spook [spuːk] v. 겁먹게 하다; 겁먹다; n. 유령, 귀신 (spooked a. 겁먹은)

If people are spooked, something has scared them or made them nervous.

복습 direction [dirékʃən] n. 방향; 지시; 위치

Direction is the way something or someone moves, faces, or is aimed.

복습 disappear [disəpíər] v. 사라지다, 보이지 않게 되다; 없어지다; 실종되다

If you say that someone or something disappears, you mean that you can no longer see them, usually because you or they have changed position.

so much for idiom ~란 게 참; ~에 대해서는 그쯤 하기로 하고

You say so much for a particular thing when you express disappointment at the fact that a situation is not as you thought it was.

복습 asleep [əslíːp] a. 잠이 든
Someone who is asleep is sleeping.

⁎ gentle [dʒentl] a. 온화한; 조심스러운; 심하지 않은 (gently ad. 약하게; 부드럽게)
If you do something gently, you do it carefully, without a lot of force or sudden change in movement.

⁎ puzzle [pʌzl] v. 어리둥절하게 하다; n. 퍼즐; 수수께끼 (puzzled a. 어리둥절한; 얼떨떨한)
If you are puzzled, you are confused because you do not understand something.

get through to idiom ~에게 이해시키다; (다음 단계로) 진출하다
If you get through to someone, you succeed in making them understand something that you are trying to tell them.

⁎ fake [feik] v. ~인 척하다; a. 가짜의, 거짓된; 모조의; n. 모조품
If you fake, you pretend to have a particular feeling or to be in a particular situation.

⁎ poke [pouk] v. (손가락 등으로) 쿡 찌르다; 쑥 내밀다; n. (손가락 등으로) 찌르기
If you poke someone or something, you quickly push them with your finger or with a sharp object.

peek [piːk] n. 엿보기; v. (재빨리) 훔쳐보다; 살짝 보이다
If you have a peek, you look at something for a short time.

⁎ scream [skriːm] v. 소리치다; 비명을 지르다, 괴성을 지르다; n. 비명, 절규
If you scream something, you shout it in a loud, high-pitched voice.

⁎ invisible [invízəbl] a. 보이지 않는, 볼 수 없는
If you describe something as invisible, you mean that it cannot be seen, for example because it is transparent, hidden, or very small.

⁎⁎⁎ face [feis] v. 향하다, 마주보다; 직면하다; n. 얼굴
If someone or something faces a particular thing, person, or direction, they are positioned opposite them or are looking in that direction.

복습 stay up idiom (늦게 까지) 안 자다, 깨어 있다
If you stay up, you remain out of bed at a time when most people have gone to bed or at a time when you are normally in bed yourself.

복습 dawn [dɔːn] n. 새벽, 여명; v. 날이 새다; 이해되기 시작하다
Dawn is the time of day when light first appears in the sky, just before the sun rises.

★ toss [tɔːs] v. (가볍게) 던지다; 흔들리다; n. 던지기
If you toss something somewhere, you throw it there lightly, often in a rather careless way.

freak [friːk] v. 기겁하다; 기겁하게 하다; n. 괴짜
If someone freaks, or if something freaks them, they suddenly feel extremely surprised, upset, angry, or confused.

★ stare [stɛər] v. 빤히 쳐다보다, 응시하다; n. 빤히 쳐다보기, 응시
If you stare at someone or something, you look at them for a long time.

make out idiom ~을 알아보다; 주장하다
If you make someone or something out, you see, hear, or understand them with difficulty.

better yet idiom 아니면, 차라리
Better yet is used when you are adding a new idea that you think is better than a good one already mentioned.

복습 groovy [grúːvi] a. 멋진, 근사한
If you describe something as groovy, you mean that it is attractive, fashionable, or exciting.

복습 at one with idiom ~와 하나가 되어
If you are at one with something, you are in a peaceful state as a part of it.

복습 universe [júːnəvəːrs] n. 우주; 은하계; (특정한 유형의) 경험 세계
A universe can be a world or an area of space that is different from the one we are in.

parallel [pǽrəlèl] a. 평행한; 아주 유사한; n. ~와 아주 유사한 것; v. ~와 유사하다
If two lines, two objects, or two lines of movement are parallel, they are the same distance apart along their whole length.

forehead [fɔ́ːrhèd] n. 이마
Your forehead is the area at the front of your head between your eyebrows and your hair.

navel [néivəl] n. 배꼽
Your navel is the small hollow just below your waist at the front of your body.

chime [ʧaim] n. 차임, 종; v. (종이나 시계가) 울리다
Chimes are a set of small objects which make a ringing sound when they are blown by the wind.

funnel [fʌnl] n. 깔때기; v. (좁은 공간 속을) 이동하다
A funnel is an object with a wide, circular top and a narrow short tube at the bottom.

pour [pɔːr] v. 붓다, 따르다; 마구 쏟아지다; 쏟아져 나오다
If you pour a liquid or other substance, you make a liquid or other substance flow out of or into a container by holding it at an angle.

bucket [bʌ́kit] n. 양동이, 들통
A bucket is a round metal or plastic container with a handle attached to its sides.

whoosh [hwuːʃ] n. 쉭 하는 소리; v. (아주 빠르게) 휙 하고 지나가다
People sometimes say 'whoosh' when they are emphasizing the fact that something happens very suddenly or very fast.

tingle [tiŋgl] v. 따끔거리다, 얼얼하다; (어떤 감정이) 마구 일다; n. 따끔거림, 얼얼함; 흥분
When a part of your body tingles, you have a slight stinging feeling there.

toe [tou] n. 발가락
Your toes are the five movable parts at the end of each foot.

* **wrist** [rist] n. 손목; 팔목
Your wrist is the part of your body between your hand and your arm
which bends when you move your hand.

* **ankle** [ǽŋkl] n. 발목
An ankle is the part at the bottom of your leg where your foot joins
your leg.

‡ **chest** [ʧest] n. 가슴, 흉부; 나무로 만든 상자
Your chest is the top part of the front of your body where your ribs,
lungs, and heart are.

복습 **lung** [lʌŋ] n. 폐, 허파
Your lungs are the two organs inside your chest which fill with air when
you breathe in.

‡ **realize** [ríːəlàiz] v. 깨닫다, 알아차리다; 실현하다, 달성하다
If you realize that something is true, you become aware of that fact or
understand it.

* **ladder** [lǽdər] n. 사다리; 단계
A ladder is a piece of equipment used for climbing up something or
down from something.

* **snap** [snæp] v. 탁 하고 움직이다; 탁 하고 부러지다; 날카롭게 말하다; n. 찰칵 하는 소리
If you snap something or if it snaps into a particular position, it moves
quickly into that position, usually with a sharp sound.

복습 **giggle** [gigl] v. 킥킥거리다; 낄낄 웃다; n. 킥킥거림; 피식 웃음
If someone giggles, they laugh in a childlike way, because they are
amused, nervous, or embarrassed.

‡ **awake** [əwéik] a. 잠이 깬, 잠들지 않은, 깨어 있는; v. (잠에서) 깨다
Someone who is awake is not sleeping.

nag [næg] v. 잔소리를 하다; 계속 괴롭히다
If someone nags you, they keep asking you to do something you have
not done yet or do not want to do.

no way idiom 절대로 안 돼; 말도 안 돼; 싫어

You can say no way for saying that you will definitely not do something or that something will definitely not happen.

1장

"잭(Zack), 너 몸 밖에 나가 본 적 있어?"

제 친구 스펜서(Spencer)가 저에게 물어본 말입니다. 그는 우리 집에서 하룻밤 자고 가기로 했습니다. 그것은 꽤나 기이한 질문이었습니다. 그렇지만 공교롭게도 저는 기이한 것에 대해 꽤 많이 알고 있습니다.

제 증조할아버지는 돌아가셨다가, 고양이로 되살아났습니다. 완다(Wanda)라는 이름의 유령은 우리 아파트를 엉망으로 만들었고요. 한번은 제가 과학 시간에 감전이 되어서, 한동안 마음을 읽을 수도 있었습니다. 오, 그리고 제 욕실 거울장 반대편에는 평행 우주가 있어요. 제가 말했듯이, 저는 기이한 것에 대해 많이 알고 있습니다.

그래도, 이 유체 이탈 이야기는 저에게 새로웠습니다. 하지만 그것은 좀 멋지게 들렸습니다. 제 친구 스펜서 샤프(Spencer Sharp)는 우리 반에서 가장 똑똑한 아이입니다. 모두가 그것을 알고 있죠, 스펜서를 포함해서요. 들리는 것처럼 그런 뜻으로 말한 것은 아닙니다. 스펜서는 아주 친절합니다. 그리고 그는 언제나 기꺼이 새로운 일을 해 보려고 합니다. 그렇지만 저는 제가 모르는 기이한 일에 대해 그가 무엇인가 알

고 있다는 것을 믿을 수 없었습니다.

"네가 네 몸 바깥에 있는지 어떻게 알아?" 제가 그에게 물었습니다.

"음, 네가 공중에 떠다니면서 너 자신을 내려다보게 되거든." 그가 말했습니다.

"하지만 내 눈은 내 몸에 있는데, 내가 무엇으로 나를 내려다볼 수 있어?" 제가 물었습니다.

"너의 영적인 몸에 있는 눈으로." 그가 말했습니다.

"그러면, 그 영적인 몸이라는 게, 정확히 뭐야?" 제가 물었습니다.

"그건 너의 일반적인 몸 안에 들어 있는 거야. 네가 그것으로 유체 이탈 여행을 할 수 있지."

새로 산 저의 이층 침대에 기댄 채, 우리는 제 침실 바닥에 앉아 있었습니다.

"넌 이걸 어떻게 알게 됐어?" 제가 물었습니다.

스펜서는 그의 책가방에서 오래된 책 한 권을 꺼내 저에게 보여 주었습니다. 초보자를 위한 영적 여행: 정신 세계를 통한 유체 이탈 여행.

"헌책방에서 이걸 샀어." 스펜서가 말했습니다. 뉴욕시(New York City)에는 헌책방이 많이 있습니다. 그리고 스펜서는 그 모든 곳에 가 본 것이 틀림없습니다. "이 책은 1960년대 거야." 그

가 말했습니다. "히피의 시대 말이야. 그건 멋진 것 같아."

"유체 이탈해서 여행하는 게 뭐가 그렇게 좋아?"

"음, 그게 비행기보다 더 빨라. 훨씬 더 싸고. 그 짜증나는 금속 탐지기를 통과하려고 줄 서 있지 않아도 되지. 그리고 절대 가방을 잃어버릴 일도 없어. 우리가 오늘 밤에 해 보면 어떨까?"

바로 그때 아빠가 제 방에 들어왔습니다. 저의 엄마와 아빠는 이혼했습니다. 저는 그들 각자와 절반씩 시간을 보냅니다.

"있지, 얘들아." 그가 말했습니다. "시간이 늦어지는구나. 오늘이 토요일인 건 알고 있어. 하지만 이제 잘 시간인 것 같구나. 너희가 서두르면, 불 끄고 30분 정도는 이야기하게 해 주마."

"알겠어요." 제가 말했습니다.

"오, 잊어버릴 뻔했구나." 아빠가 말했습니다. "방금 부엌에서 쥐 한 마리를 봤어. 그러니 그곳에 간식을 가지러 가면, 손님이 있을 수도 있단다."

아빠가 떠나고, 스펜서와 저는 잠옷을 입었습니다. 그리고 나서 우리는 침대로 기어 올라갔습니다. 스펜서가 손님이었기 때문에 위층을 썼습니다. 그게 아빠가 저에게 이층 침대를 사 준 진짜 이유입니다―친구들이 자고 가고요.

"그래서 어떻게 생각해, 잭?" 불을 끄자 스펜서가 물었습니다. "너 오늘 밤에 유체 이탈 여행을 해 보고 싶니?"

"모르겠어." 제가 말했습니다. "그런 것 같아."

그는 손전등을 켰고 그의 유체 이탈 책을 펼쳤습니다. 그는 소리 내어 읽기 시작했습니다: "근사한 시간을 보낼 준비를 하세요. 먼저, 눈을 감고 누우세요. 풍경이 있다면, 풍경 소리를 들어 보세요. 우주와 하나가 되세요. 그런 뒤 왼손을 당신의 이마 위에 얹으세요. 바로 한가운데에. 물병자리 시대 사람들은 이것을 제3의 눈이라고 부르지요. 그다음 오른손을 배꼽 위에 올립니다. . . ."

"책에 진짜로 배꼽이라고 쓰여 있어?"

"탯줄이 있던 자리라고 했어, 알겠니? 네가 그 단어를 아는지 몰랐어."

스펜서는 평소에는 거만하게 굴지 않습니다. 하지만 그가 그럴 때 저는 그것이 정말 싫습니다. "해석해 줘서 고맙네." 제가 말했습니다.

"이제 당신의 영적인 몸이 진짜 몸 밖으로 천천히 스며 나오게 하세요. . . 탯줄이 있던 자리를 통해서요. 됐니?" 스펜서가 저를 힐끗 쳐다봤습니다. 그러고 나서 그는 계속해서 읽었습니다. "연기처럼 스며 나와서 당신의 몸 위로 떠오릅니다. . . ."

저는 그 책이 말한 대로 하려고 했어요. 효과가 있는 것 같지 않았습니다.

"너도 이 일을 모두 하고 있는 거야?" 제가 물었습니다.

"물론이지." 스펜서가 말했습니다. 스펜서는 "물론이지"라고 말하는 것을 무척 좋아합니다.

"그러면 그게 너한테는 효과가 있어?" 제가 물었습니다.

"아직 모르겠어." 그가 말했습니다.

그 말은 아니라는 뜻입니다. "그냥 계속해 봐." 그가 말했습니다. "때로는 시간이 좀 걸려. 특히 처음에는."

"넌 이거 엄청 많이 해 봤어?" 제가 물었습니다.

"아니, 그렇게 많이는 안 해 봤어."

"한 번 이상?"

"어, 아니. 더 적게."

우리는 약 한 시간 동안 그것을 해 봤습니다. 아무 일도 일어나지 않았습니다. 저는 스펜서에게 그가 저에게 올바른 지시사항을 주지 못하는 게 틀림없다고 말했습니다. 그는 제가 그것들을 제대로 따라 하지 않는 게 틀림없다고 말했습니다. 하지만 마찬가지로, 그에게도 아무런 일이 일어나지 않았습니다.

그런데 그때, 마침내, 저는 뭔가를 느꼈습니다. 제 배꼽 위에 있는 손에서 간

지러움이 약간 느껴졌어요. "스며 나와라. . . . 스며 나와라." 저는 제 영적인 몸에게 계속해서 말했습니다.

몇 분 뒤 저는 제 손에서 또 다른 간지러움을 느꼈습니다. 이번에는 그것이 숨결처럼 느껴졌습니다. 저는 눈을 떴습니다. 저는 거의 제 몸 밖으로 빠져나와 있었습니다! 하지만 제 다리가 끼어 있었습니다. 저는 유사(流沙) 안에 있는 것처럼 느껴졌습니다. 저는 당기고 또 당겼습니다. 갑자기 그것이 탁 하고 빠져나왔습니다! 그리고 그다음 저는 공중을 떠다니고 있었어요! 천장 가까이에서 위아래로 움직이고 있었어요!

2장

"스펜서!" 저는 소리쳤습니다. "나 천장에 있어!"

저는 아래를 봤습니다. 저는 제 몸을 볼 수 있었습니다. 제 몸은 여전히 침대 위에 누워 있었습니다. 제 두 눈은 감겨 있었습니다. 왼손은 여전히 이마 위에 있었습니다. 오른손은 여전히 배꼽 위에 있었습니다.

이상했어요! 다른 사람들이 저를 보듯이 제가 저 자신을 보고 있었습니다.

침대 위층에 누워 있는, 스펜서가 보였습니다. 그의 눈은 감겨 있었습니다.

그는 움직이지 않았습니다. 그가 자고 있는 걸까요, 아니면 뭘까요?

"야, 스펜서!" 제가 불렀습니다. "너 그 안에 있어?"

"아니!" 제 바로 뒤에서 어떤 목소리가 말했습니다. "나 여기에 나와 있어!"

저는 고개를 돌렸습니다.

스펜서가 바로 제 옆에서 천장 가까이 위아래로 둥실거리고 있었습니다! 그는 거의 똑같아 보였습니다. 그가 좀 투명해 보인다는 점만 빼면요. 그리고 그는 약간 반짝이는 것처럼 보였습니다.

"우리가 해냈어!" 제가 말했습니다. "우리가 진짜로 우리 몸을 빠져나왔어!"

"물론이지." 스펜서가 말했습니다. 마치 그가 매일 밤 그렇게 했다는 듯이 말입니다.

놀라웠어요. 제 몸이 공기보다 더 가볍게 느껴졌습니다. 제 몸은 무게가 전혀 나가지 않는 것처럼 느껴졌습니다. 몸이 없는 것처럼 느껴졌습니다.

돌아다니는 것이 재미있었습니다. 저는 제가 숨을 내쉬면, 가라앉기 시작한다는 것을 알아냈습니다. 하지만 숨을 들이마시면, 저는 떠올랐습니다. 앞으로 가기 위해서는, 마치 헤엄치는 것처럼, 두 팔과 두 다리를 움직이기만 하면 되었습니다. 공중에서 헤엄치는 거죠.

재미 삼아, 저는 공중제비를 돌았습니다.

"이거 엄청 멋지다." 제가 말했습니다.

"그래서 너는 어디로 여행하고 싶니?" 스펜서가 물었습니다.

"모르겠어." 제가 말했습니다. "우리가 어디에 갈 수 있을까?"

"우리가 원하는 곳은 어디든지." 스펜서가 말했습니다. 그는 자신의 얼굴에 반짝거리는 환한 웃음을 지어 보였습니다.

"우리 아빠의 서재에 들어가 보는 건 어때?" 제가 말했습니다.

"나는 오히려 이집트(Egypt) 같은 곳을 생각하고 있었는데." 스펜서가 말했습니다.

스펜서는 이집트에 관한 지리 프로젝트를 막 끝냈습니다. 그는 각설탕 743개로 피라미드(pyramid)를 만들었습니다. 그것은 꽤 멋졌습니다.

"이집트에서 우리가 뭘 할 건데?" 제가 물었습니다.

"글쎄." 스펜서가 말했습니다. "나일 강(Nile)을 따라가는 거야. 피라미드도 보고."

"멋지다!" 제가 말했습니다. "그런데 우리가 거기까지 가는 데 오래 걸릴까?"

"아마도." 스펜서가 말했습니다. "이집트는 5,000마일(mile, 약 8,046킬로미터)도 더 떨어져 있어."

"음, 우리는 아침까지는 돌아와야 해." 제가 말했습니다. "그렇지 않으면 아빠가 걱정하실 거야. 집에서 좀 더 가까운 곳을 고르자. 브롱크스 동물원(Bronx Zoo)은 어때?"

"동물원 좋지." 스펜서가 말했습니다.

저는 문 쪽으로 둥둥 날아갔습니다. 문은 닫혀 있었습니다. 저는 그것을 열 수 없었습니다. 저는 문손잡이를 잡을 수도 없었습니다. 저는 창문으로 둥둥 떠서 날아갔습니다. 창문도 닫혀 있었습니다.

"여기서 우리가 어떻게 나갈 수 있을까?" 제가 물었습니다.

"벽을 통과해서 가면 어때?" 스펜서가 말했습니다.

"그리고 내가 그걸 어떻게 할 수 있는데?" 제가 물었습니다.

"이렇게." 스펜서가 말했습니다.

그는 두 손을 모아서 자기 머리 위로 올렸습니다. 그는 자신의 두 다리로 가위 차기를 했습니다. 그는 제 침실 벽으로 휙 움직였습니다. 그의 두 손이 사라졌습니다. 그다음 그의 머리가 사라졌습니다. 그다음 그의 몸의 남은 부분들도요. 스펜서는 벽이 마치 젤로(Jell-O)라도 되는 것처럼 미끄러지듯 벽을 통과했습니다.

굉장하네요!

"야! 기다려!" 제가 소리쳤습니다.

저는 제 두 손을 모으고 밀어서 나아갔습니다. 제 머리가 벽을 통과했습니다. 저는 나무와 벽돌이 휙 지나치는 것을 보았습니다. 아무것도 느껴지지 않았습니다.

그리고 그다음 저는 밖으로 나왔습니다.

이크!

저는 30층 높이에 있었습니다!

제 발밑에 공기 말고는 아무것도 없었습니다! 저 멀리 제 아래로 도시의 작은 불빛들이 있었습니다.

사람 살려!

3장

저는 어쩔 줄을 몰랐습니다. 공기가 제 폐 바깥으로 빠져나갔습니다. 저는 떨어지기 시작했습니다. 그때 저는 숨을 들이마셔야 한다는 것을 기억했습니다. 그리고 저는 다시 위로 떠올랐습니다. 킥킥거리면서, 스펜서가 저를 기다리고 있었습니다.

"그래서, 우리 이제 동물원으로 가는 거야?" 그가 물었습니다.

"날 따라와." 제가 말했습니다.

우리는 이스트 52번가(East 52nd Street)에 있는 아빠의 집을 떠났습니다. 우리는 도심을 벗어나 날아갔습니다. . . 높은 건물들 꼭대기를 지나. . . 파크 애비뉴(Park Avenue)를 지나. . . 양쪽으로 이동하는 자동차들의 행렬을 지나. . . 그리고 나서 센트럴 파크(Central Park) 너머로 나아갔습니다. 저는 슈퍼맨(Superman)이 된 기분이었습니다. 슈퍼맨 영화에 나오는 음악이 들리는 것 같았습니다.

"이거 정말 멋지다, 안 그래?" 스펜서가 소리쳤습니다.

"최고로 멋져!" 저도 되받아 소리쳤습니다.

잠시 후 우리는 브롱크스 동물원 위를 날고 있었습니다.

"신사 숙녀 여러분." 제가 말했습니다. "저는 여러분의 기장입니다. 우리는 곧 브롱크스 동물원에 착륙할 예정입니다. 좌석 안전벨트가 단단히 채워져 있는지 확인하시기 바랍니다. 그리고 여러분의 좌석 등받이와 접이식 테이블은 똑바로 세워 고정해 주시기 바랍니다."

우리는 땅을 향해 둥둥 떠서 내려갔습니다.

"신사 숙녀 여러분." 저는 계속 말했습니다. "브롱크스 동물원에 도착했습니다. 행복한 저녁 보내시기 바랍니다. 유체 이탈 항공사를 이용해 주셔서 감사합니다. 우리 마일리지 프로그램을 이용하시는 고객님께는, 오늘 밤 비행으로 15마일이 적립됩니다."

동물원은 닫혀 있었습니다. 사람이 아무도 없었습니다—스펜서와 저를 제외하고는요. 그런데, 생각해 보니, 우리가 사람으로 여겨질 수 있는지 저는 잘 모르겠어요. 그곳은 아주 어두웠습니다. 그리고 멀리에서 늑대 같은 어떤 동물이 우는 소리를 들을 수 있었습니다.

"이곳은 밤에 오니까 훨씬 더 으스스하구나." 스펜서가 말했습니다.

저는 고개를 끄덕였습니다. "하지만 일단 여기 왔으니까, 사자를 보러 가자." 제가 말했습니다. 저는 사자에 푹 빠져 있습니다.

우리는 사자가 있는 구역으로 갔습니다. 사자는 한 마리도 볼 수 없었습니다.

"그래서, 그것들은 다 어디에 있지?" 제가 물었습니다.

"자러 갔겠지, 틀림없어." 스펜서가 말했습니다. "밤이잖아."

"그럼 그것들은 틀림없이 저 동굴 바로 안에 있을 거야." 제가 말했습니다. "가서 한번 보자."

"잭, 너 미쳤어?"

"스펜서, 우리는 몸 밖에 나와 있잖아."

"그리고 너는 정신도 나갔지."

"하지만 우리가 우리 몸 안에 있는

게 아니라면 말이야." 제가 말했습니다. "사자들이 우리를 다치게 할 수 없잖아. 맞지?"

스펜서는 그 말의 논리를 이해한 것 같았습니다.

"가자!" 제가 말했습니다.

우리는 동굴 안으로 둥둥 떠서 날아갔습니다. 아무것도 볼 수 없었습니다. 하지만 코 고는 소리는 들을 수 있었습니다. 이상한 소리였습니다. 수많은 커다란 야옹이들이, 어둠 속에서 코를 골고 있었습니다. 그때 그것들 중 하나가 기침을 했습니다. 네, 반은 기침이었고 반은 으르렁거리는 소리였습니다.

"잭." 스펜서가 제 바로 옆에서 속삭였습니다. "이건 정말 멍청한 생각이야."

"왜?"

"왜냐고? 왜냐면 말이지. 그것들이 깰 수도 있잖아. 그리고 그것들이 우리의 영적인 엉덩이를 물어 버리려고 할 수도 있다고."

"흐으으으음. 어쩌면 네 말에 일리가 있겠다." 제가 말했습니다.

제가 길을 앞장서며, 우리는 다시 동굴 입구를 향해 둥둥 날아갔습니다.

우리의 영적인 눈은 어둠에 익숙해진 것이 틀림없었습니다. 아니면 동굴 입구가 더 밝았던 것일지도 모르고요. 왜냐하면 우리가 그쪽에 갔을 때, 우리 앞에 서 있는 커다란 사자를 보는 게 전혀 어렵지 않았거든요.

그것은 제가 본 것 중에 가장 큰 사자였습니다. 아니면 그냥 제가 이전에는 사자를 그렇게 가까이에서 본 적이 없었던 것일지도 모르고요.

"어-어쩌면 사자가 우리를 모-못 볼 수도 있어." 스펜서가 속삭였습니다.

저는 손을 들어서 살짝 흔들었습니다. 사자는 알아채지 못하는 것처럼 보였습니다. 저는 제 양팔을 흔들어 보았습니다. 사자가 그의 입을 벌렸습니다. 그리고 하품했습니다.

"우리를 못 봐!" 제가 말했습니다.

그래서 저는 사자 쪽으로 움직였습니다.

이상하네요! 이번에는 사자가 한 발짝 뒤로 물러섰습니다.

저는 조금 더 가까이 다가갔습니다. 사자가 더 멀리 물러섰습니다.

"와! 그는 우리가 여기 있다는 게 느껴지나 봐." 스펜서가 속삭였습니다.

"그리고 그가 우리를 무서워하고 있어!" 제가 큰 소리로 말했습니다.

사자가 한 발짝 앞으로 나왔습니다. 그리고 으르렁거렸습니다.

"좋아." 제가 말했습니다. "그러니까 그는 우리를 무서워하지는 않는구나."

"우리는 여기서 나가야 해." 스펜서가 속삭였습니다.

"스펜서." 제가 말했습니다. "날 따라

와!"

저는 몇 피트(feet) 정도 뒤로 물러섰습니다. 저는 제 두 손을 모으고 사자 오른쪽에 있는 빈 공간으로 다이빙했습니다.

이런! 사자가 오른쪽으로 움직였습니다. 그리고 그의 입을 벌렸습니다. 아주 크게요.

저는 멈추려고 했습니다. 전 멈출 수가 없었어요. 저는 곧장 사자의 입속으로 뛰어들었고, 스펜서가 바로 뒤따라왔습니다.

4장

우리는 사자의 입을 통과했습니다. 그의 몸을 통해서 미끄러져 나왔어요. 우리는 탈출했습니다!

잠시 후 우리는 위로 쌩 하고 날아올라 브롱크스 동물원을 떠났습니다.

"우리 이제 어디로 가는 거야?" 스펜서가 외쳤습니다.

"알게 될 거야!" 제가 말했습니다.

브루클린(Brooklyn)의 코니아일랜드(Coney Island)에 있는 놀이공원은 동물원만큼이나 어둡고 사람이 없었습니다. 롤러코스터(roller-coaster) 경사로의 튀어나온 부분이 공룡 뼈처럼 보였

습니다. 그것은 아주 기묘한 느낌으로, 멋졌습니다.

스펜서는 곧장 롤러코스터를 타고 싶어 했습니다. 물론, 열차는 운행하지 않았습니다. 그래서 우리는 열차 없이 롤러코스터를 타기로 했습니다. 거꾸로 언덕을 떨어져 내려가는 것은 정말 재미있었습니다. 하지만 여러분이 몸 바깥에 나와 있는 게 아니라면, 해 보라고 추천하지는 않습니다.

우리의 다음 목적지는 자유의 여신상(Statue of Liberty)이었습니다. 저는 언제나 그 맨 꼭대기에 가 보고 싶었습니다. 하지만 절대로 줄을 서거나 그 계단을 전부 올라가고 싶지는 않았습니다. 스펜서와 저는 횃불의 꼭대기로 날아갔습니다. 전망이 아주 멋졌습니다.

그때 좋은 생각이 났습니다. 저는 자유의 여신상의 코 바로 아래로 날아갔습니다.

"내가 뭔지 맞혀 봐!" 저는 스펜서에게 소리쳤습니다.

"모르겠어."

"영적인 코딱지야!"

그런 뒤 우리는 다시 도시 외곽으로 향했습니다. 타임스 스퀘어(Times Square) 근처 브로드웨이(Broadway)에서, 우리는 블록을 둘러싸고 늘어서 있는 긴 줄을 보았습니다. 터미네이터 3000(Terminator 3000)

이 막 개봉했습니다. 우리의 부모님들 중 누구도 우리가 그 영화를 보는 것을 좋아하지 않았습니다. 거의 백만 명의 사람이 온갖 끔찍한 방법으로 죽게 되거든요.

"지금이 기회야!" 스펜서가 말했습니다.

그래서 우리는 날아서 내려갔습니다. 우리는 줄을 서 있는 모든 사람들을 지나갔습니다. 그리고, 당연히, 돈을 낼 필요도 없었죠!

팝콘에서 아주 좋은 냄새가 났습니다. 저는 팝콘 한 봉지를 먹으려고 다가갔습니다. 하지만 그때 생각이 났어요. 저는 아무것도 먹을 수 없었습니다. 실망이네요!

스펜서는 로비에서 많은 비디오게임을 보고 있었습니다. 멋진 것들이 많이 있었습니다. 하지만 매번 우리가 조종기를 잡으려고 할 때마다, 우리의 영적인 손은 그것들을 통과해서 미끄러질 뿐이었습니다.

그래서 우리는 영화가 시작하기를 기다렸습니다. 평소에 저는 키가 7피트(feet, 약 213센티미터)쯤 되는 사람 뒤에서 꼼짝도 못 하곤 합니다. 이번에는, 아무 문제 없었습니다. 스펜서와 저는 저 위 천장 가까이에서 완벽하게 잘 보였거든요.

문제는, 우리가 생각했던 것보다 영화가 훨씬 더 무서웠다는 점이었습니다. 저는 스펜서를 쳐다봤습니다. 그도 저를 쳐다봤습니다.

"우리 이제 집으로 돌아가야 할 것 같아." 제가 말했습니다.

"왜?" 스펜서가 말했습니다.

"왜냐하면 말이지." 제가 말했습니다. "나는 좀 자야 하거든. 집에 가서 자지 않으면, 나는 내일 엉망이 될 거야."

"너 집에서 자는 중이야." 스펜서가 말했습니다. "적어도 네 몸은 말이야. 네 나머지 부분은 네가 원하는 만큼 늦게까지 깨어 있어도 돼."

"그래도 우리는 집에 가야 할 것 같아." 제가 말했습니다.

"어, 알았어." 스펜서가 말했습니다.

저는 우리 모험에서 가장 무서운 일이 우리를 기다리고 있다는 것을 전혀 모르고 있었습니다!

5장

우리가 아빠의 아파트로 돌아와서 벽을 통해 제 방 안으로 미끄러져 들어왔을 때는, 시간이 정말 늦어 있었습니다. 저는 자러 가고 싶었습니다. 그럴 필요가 없었는데도 말이죠. 이상하죠, 그렇죠?

"좋아, 스펜서." 제가 말했습니다. "우

리 몸으로 어떻게 되돌아가는 거야?"

"그렇게 하는 방법은 여러 가지가 있어." 그가 말했습니다.

"우리는 어떤 방법을 써야 해?"

"어, 아마도 책에 나와 있는 방법이겠지."

"그래서 책에 뭐라고 나와 있어?"

"음, 여기 한번 보자."

그는 책이 있는 쪽으로 날아갔는데, 책은 위층 침대에 누워 있는 그의 몸 옆에 있었습니다.

"어때?" 제가 말했습니다.

"작은 문제가 생긴 것 같아." 그가 말했습니다.

"무슨 작은 문제?"

"책이 13페이지에 펼쳐져 있어." 그가 말했습니다. "우리가 몸 밖으로 나오는 내용에 대한 페이지야. 다시 들어가는 방법은 다음 장에 있어. 14페이지에."

"그럼, 책장을 넘겨."

스펜서가 저를 바라봤습니다.

"오, 안 돼." 제가 말했습니다. 저는 저의 영적인 손으로 영적인 이마를 탁 쳤습니다. "책장을 못 넘기는구나."

"내가 내 몸 안에 있으면 넘길 수 있겠지." 그가 말했습니다.

"네가 네 몸 안에 있다면, 그럴 필요가 없겠지." 제가 말했습니다.

"맞아."

"우리가 우리 몸 안으로 돌아가지 못하면 우리는 어떻게 하지?" 제가 말했습니다.

스펜서는 초조해하며 어깨를 으쓱했습니다. 그것이 저를 겁먹게 했습니다. 스펜서는 어떤 문제에 대해서든 언제나 정답을 알고 있습니다. 하지만 이번에는 아니었습니다.

"어쩌면 아빠가 우리를 도와줄 수 있을지도 몰라." 제가 말했습니다.

저는 제 침실 문을 통과해 헤엄쳐서 아빠의 침실로 떠서 들어갔습니다. 스펜서도 저를 따라왔습니다.

아빠는 깊이 잠들어 있었습니다. 한쪽 다리가 침대 밖으로 나와 늘어져 있었습니다. 그의 눈은 감겨 있었습니다. 그의 입은 벌어져 있었습니다. 그리고 그는 베개에 침을 좀 흘리고 있었습니다.

"아빠!" 제가 소리쳤습니다. "일어나세요!"

그는 계속 자기만 했습니다.

저는 그의 머리 쪽으로 떠올라서 갔습니다. 그의 귀에 입술을 바짝 가져다 댔습니다.

"아빠! 일어나세요! 문제가 생겼어요!"

아빠는 정말 잠을 깊이 자는 편입니다. 그는 조금도 움직이지 않았습니다.

"스펜서." 제가 말했습니다. "아빠는 일어나지 않을 거야."

"그래 보여." 스펜서가 말했습니다. 그는 제 바로 옆에 떠 있었습니다. 그는 잠시 생각했습니다. 그러더니 그가 말했습니다. "콜먼-레빈 선생님(Mrs. Coleman-Levin) 댁에 가 보는 건 어때?"

"그게 무슨 도움이 되는데?" 제가 물었습니다.

콜먼-레빈 선생님은 우리 과학 선생님이자 담임 선생님입니다. 그녀도 좀 기이한 편입니다. 그녀는 병에 담긴 돼지 뇌를 책상 위에 둡니다. 잘 차려입어야 하는 파티에서조차, 그녀는 작업용 부츠를 신습니다. 그리고 그녀는 주말에 시체 안치소에서 부검을 합니다. 그 말은 그녀가 사람들이 무엇 때문에 죽었는지 알아보기 위해 시체를 조각조각 잘라 본다는 말입니다. 웩!

"선생님은 기이한 것에 대해 많이 아시잖아." 스펜서가 말했습니다. "선생님이 도와주실지도 몰라. 그리고 선생님이 새벽까지 자지 않고 깨어 있다는 걸 내가 마침 알고 있거든."

더 좋은 생각이 떠오르지 않았습니다. 그래서 저는 말했습니다. "안 될 것 없지?"

스펜서는 콜먼-레빈 선생님의 집으로 가는 길을 알고 있었습니다. 그는 어느 방학 때 그녀의 커다란 파리지옥풀에게 살아 있는 곤충을 잡아서 먹이는

것으로 추가 점수를 받았습니다. 그는 동네 건너편에 있는 선생님의 아파트로 길을 안내했습니다.

콜먼-레빈 선생님의 아파트는 아주 멋졌습니다. 그곳은 마치 열대 우림처럼 보였습니다. 거대한 야자나무와 수많은 열대 식물과 늘어져 있는 덩굴 식물 같은 것들이 있었습니다. 심지어 조그만 폭포도 있었습니다. 그리고, 물론, 파리지옥풀도요.

우리는 콜먼-레빈 선생님의 방을 찾았습니다. 그녀는 침대에 있었습니다. 깊이 잠들어 있었습니다. 작업용 부츠를 신은 채로요.

"스펜서, 선생님이 새벽까지 깨어 계신다고 네가 말했던 것 같은데." 제가 말했습니다. "아직 새벽도 안 됐는걸."

"그럼 내가 틀렸나 봐." 스펜서가 말했습니다.

"아니면 그녀가 아직 깨어 있거나." 또 다른 목소리가 말했습니다.

그 목소리는 위쪽에서 들려왔습니다. 우리는 위를 올려다봤습니다.

콜먼-레빈 선생님이 천장 가까이에서 책상다리를 하고 앉아 있었습니다!

6장

"콜먼-레빈 선생님! 유체 이탈을 하셨

네요!" 저는 소리쳤습니다.

"아주 대단한 관찰력이구나, 잭." 그녀가 말했습니다.

"그런데 어떻게 하셨어요?" 스펜서가 물었습니다.

"너희는 어떻게 했니?" 그녀가 말했습니다.

"저희는 책에서 배웠어요." 제가 말했습니다.

"책이 배우기 좋지." 그녀가 말했습니다. "몸 밖으로 나와서 어디에 가 봤니?"

"브롱크스 동물원하고요." 제가 말했습니다. "그리고 코니아일랜드요. 그리고 자유의 여신상이요. 영화관에도 갔어요."

"너희 아주 바쁜 밤을 보낸 것 같구나." 그녀가 말했습니다.

"그랬어요." 스펜서가 말했습니다.

"나는 왜 찾아온 거니?"

"우리 몸 안으로 돌아가는 방법을 몰라서요." 스펜서가 말했습니다. "선생님은 방법을 알지도 모른다고 생각했어요."

"나야 물론 알지." 그녀가 말했습니다.

"잘됐네요!" 제가 말했습니다. "저희에게 알려 주실 거죠?"

"당연히 아니지." 그녀가 미소를 지으며 말했습니다.

"왜 안 알려 주세요?" 제가 말했습니다.

"왜냐하면 말이야. 내가 너희에게 말하면, 너희는 아무것도 배울 수 없거든. 스스로 알아내면, 배우는 것이 있을 거야."

"저희는 그 책에서 알아낼 수도 있었어요." 스펜서가 말했습니다. "하지만 책은 13페이지에 펼쳐져 있어요. 그리고 몸 안으로 돌아가는 방법은 14페이지에 있어요. 저희는 책장을 넘길 수가 없고요."

"그렇다면 나는 너희에게 실험을 해보는 걸 추천할게." 그녀가 말했습니다. 콜먼-레빈 선생님은 실험을 굉장히 좋아합니다. "그리고 장담하는데 너희는 해결책을 알아낼 거야."

콜먼-레빈 선생님은 손을 흔들어 인사했습니다. 우리가 떠나야 한다는 뜻 같았습니다.

"저희에게 아무것도 말해 주지 않으실 건가요?" 제가 물었습니다.

"어머, 알려 줘야지." 그녀가 말했습니다. "몸 안에 있는 사람은 아무도 너희를 보지 못한다는 걸 말해 줄게. 듣지도 못하고. 하지만 너희 둘 다 똑똑한 아이들이잖니. 그러니 영적인 머리를 써 보렴. 너희가 몸에 들어가지 못해서 월요일 아침 8시 30분 정각에 수업에 오지 않으면, 나는 너희를 결석으로 표시해야 하거든. 그리고 나는 정말 그렇게 하고 싶지 않단다!"

7장

우리가 아빠의 아파트에 돌아왔을 때는, 일요일 아침이었습니다. 스펜서와 저 둘 다 몸 바깥에 나와 있는 것에 질렸습니다. 벽을 통과하고 도시 위로 날아다니는 것이 재미있는 만큼, 손으로 목을 긁을 수 있다는 것도 멋진 일입니다. 또는 침대 속에 폭 파고드는 일도요. 아니면 아침 식사로 베이글과 크림치즈를 먹는 일이요. 저는 제가 그런 단순한 것들을 그리워할 거라고는 전혀 생각하지 못했습니다.

우리는 제 방으로 헤엄쳐 갔습니다. 거기에 우리가 있었습니다—침대 위층과 아래층에요. 우리가 우리의 몸을 남겨 둔 그 자리에 말이에요.

"이제 우리 어떻게 하지?" 제가 물었습니다.

"모르겠어." 스펜서가 말했습니다. "입을 통해서 네 몸 안으로 기어 들어가는 것은 어때?"

저는 제 몸 쪽으로 날아갔습니다.

"내 입이 다물어져 있어." 제가 말했습니다.

"음, 그거 의외네." 스펜서가 말했습니다.

저는 그를 쏘아봤습니다.

스펜서는 그의 몸 쪽으로 날아가서 자기 몸을 바라봤습니다.

"내 입도 다물어져 있어." 그가 말했습니다. "있지, 콧구멍을 통해서 네 몸을 집어넣는 것은 어때?"

저는 제 몸을 바라보고는 고개를 가로저었습니다.

"난 저기에 손가락 하나 이상은 못 넣어." 제가 말했습니다.

"난 벌써 네가 하나 이상 넣는 걸 본 적이 있는데." 스펜서가 말했습니다.

저는 그의 영적인 팔을 주먹으로 쳤습니다. 주먹은 그의 팔을 바로 통과해서 반대편으로 빠져나가갔습니다.

갑자기 무언가 털로 덮인 작은 것이 침대 위층을 가로질러 날쌔게 지나갔습니다. 그러더니 그것은 벽을 타고 내려와서 침대 아래층에서 멈춰 섰습니다.

"으악!" 제가 말했습니다. "쥐잖아!"

"너 쥐가 무섭니?" 스펜서가 말했습니다. "너는 사자 입에 뛰어들었던 녀석이잖아."

"그냥 놀란 거야, 그게 다야." 제가 말했습니다. "스펜서, 우리가 다시 몸 안으로 돌아갈 방법을 찾지 못하면 어떡하지?"

"그러면 월요일 아침에 콜먼-레빈 선

생님이 우리를 결석으로 표시하시겠지." 스펜서가 말했습니다.

"콜먼-레빈 선생님은 신경 쓰지 마." 제가 말했습니다. "한 시간쯤 있으면, 우리 아빠가 아침 먹으라고 우리를 깨우러 여기로 오실 거야. 우리를 깨우지 못하면, 그가 뭐라고 생각하겠어?"

"우리가 의식불명이라고 생각하시겠지." 스펜서가 말했습니다.

저는 고개를 끄덕였습니다. 아빠는 그런 것에 잘 대처하지 못할 것입니다.

"우리는 뭔가 생각해 내야 해." 제가 말했습니다. "스펜서, 너는 천재잖아. 뭔가 생각해 봐!"

"흐으으으음. 어쩌면 우리 과학적 방법을 시도해 봐야 할지도 모르겠다." 스펜서가 제안했습니다. 과학적인 방법은 콜먼-레빈 선생님이 언제나 이야기하시는 또 다른 것이었습니다. 그것은 진짜 과학자들이 문제를 해결하는 방법입니다.

"그러는 편이 좋겠어." 제가 말했습니다.

"과학적 방법 1단계는 관찰하는 거야." 스펜서가 말했습니다. "음, 나는 우리가 우리 힘으로 저 책의 책장을 넘길 방법은 없다는 것을 알겠어."

여기까지는 저도 그와 같은 생각이었습니다.

"2단계는 가설을 세우는 거야." 스펜서가 말을 이어 갔습니다.

"알겠어." 제가 말했습니다.

"나에게는 우리가 누군가에게 우리를 위해 저 책장을 넘기게 할 수 있을 거라는 가설이 있어." 스펜서가 말했습니다.

"그러면 누구야, 정확히, 네가 생각하는 사람이?" 제가 말했습니다.

바로 그때 그 쥐가 제 침대 아래에서 다시 나타났습니다. 쥐는 러그를 가로질러서 날쌔게 달려갔습니다.

"쥐야, 당연히." 스펜서가 말했습니다.

"쥐?" 제가 말했습니다.

스펜서는 제가 의아해한다는 것을 알아챘습니다.

"잭, 동물들은 우리를 볼 수는 없어." 그가 말했습니다. "하지만 그 사자는 분명 우리를 감지하는 것 같았어."

"맞아." 제가 말했습니다. "하지만 그게 뭐?"

"그러니까." 스펜서가 말했습니다. "어쩌면 우리가 쥐를 책 옆으로 몰 수도 있잖아. 쥐가 책장을 가로질러 가게 해서 그걸 넘길 수 있을지도 몰라."

흐으으으음. 글쎄요, 그건 승산이 거의 없는 일이었습니다. 하지만 지금으로서는 그것이 우리가 가진 전부였습니다.

"좋아." 제가 말했습니다. "한번 그렇게 해 보자구."

"3단계: 가설을 시험한다." 스펜서가 말했습니다.

그래서 우리는 그렇게 했습니다. 쥐가 제 곰 인형을 갉아먹기 시작했습니다. 저는 그것이 조금도 좋지 않았습니다. 저는 제 곰 인형 쪽으로 날아갔습니다. 쥐가 올려다봤습니다.

"안녕, 생쥐야." 제가 말했습니다. 제가 왜 쥐에게 말을 걸고 있는지는 몰라도, 그렇게 했습니다. "너는 우리를 볼 수 없지만, 우리는 여기에 있단다. 우리는 남자아이들이야. 생쥐를 좋아하는 남자아이들. 네가 우리를 좀 도와줬으면 해. 그저 침대 위층으로 올라가 주기만 하면 돼. 그리고 저 책을 가로질러서 달려가 줘. 그리고 우리를 위해 책장을 넘겨 주는 거야."

쥐는 혼란스러워 보였습니다. 그는 겁먹은 것처럼 보였습니다. 그는 저에게서 뒤로 물러났습니다.

좋았어! 그가 맞는 방향으로 움직이고 있었습니다. 그는 침대 위층으로 쪼르르 올라갔습니다. 책 쪽으로요. 하지만 그다음 그는 책을 지나쳐서 벽을 타고 바닥 쪽으로 내려갔습니다. 그리고 그런 뒤 그는 사라졌습니다.

"에잇!" 제가 말했습니다.

"과학적 방법은 이쯤에서 그만두자." 스펜서가 말했습니다.

바로 그때 제 침실 문이 열렸습니다.

아빠가 불쑥 머리를 밀어 넣었습니다. 그는 이층 침대 쪽을 바라봤습니다.

맙소사, 아빠를 보자 저는 너무 기뻤습니다!

"아빠!" 그가 우리의 말을 들을 수 없다는 것을 잊은 채, 저는 소리쳤습니다. "저희에게 문제가 생겼어요! 저희는 아빠 도움이 정말 필요해요!"

"이런, 이 녀석들 자고 있으니 정말 귀엽네." 아빠가 말했습니다.

"아니에요, 아빠! 우리 안 자요! 우리는 귀엽지 않아요! 우리는 여기 위에 있어요!" 제가 소리쳤습니다.

"좋은 아침이다, 얘들아." 아빠가 말했습니다. "아침으로 딸기잼 바른 와플 먹고 싶은 사람?"

"아빠!" 제가 말했습니다. "우리를 도와주셔야 해요!"

아빠는 침대 쪽으로 걸어갔습니다. 그는 제 어깨를 잡고 제 몸을 살짝 흔들었습니다.

"일어나렴, 잭." 그가 말했습니다.

"아빠! 저 안 자요! 저는 지금 제 몸 안에 없어요!"

"잭?"

아빠는 어리둥절한 것 같았습니다.

"아빠! 아빠는 어떻게 해야 이해하시겠어요?"

"잭, 무슨 일이니? 자는 척하는 거니?"

아빠는 일어서서 스펜서를 쿡 찔러 봤습니다. 그때 아빠가 책을 봤습니다. 유체 이탈 책 말이에요. 그는 그것을 집어 들고 쳐다봤습니다.

"이게 뭐야. . . ? 초보자를 위한 영적 여행?"

"네! 맞아요! 아빠가 알아낼 거야, 스펜서! 우리 아빠가 알아낼 거라고!"

아빠는 책의 내용을 빠르게 훑어봤습니다.

"흐으으으음." 아빠가 말했습니다. "너희는 몸을 떠나는 방법을 알아냈니?"

"그랬어요!" 제가 외쳤습니다. "네! 우리가 한 게 바로 그거예요!"

"너희가 몸을 떠난 거라면." 아빠가 말했습니다. "아마도 너희는 눈에 보이지 않겠구나. . . ."

"네, 아빠! 그래요!" 제가 소리쳤습니다. "그래요!"

"너희가 내 얼굴 바로 앞을 떠다니고 있을 수도 있겠구나. 그리고 나는 너희를 볼 수 없고. . . ."

"네!" 제가 소리쳤습니다. "맞아요!"

"너희가 심지어 나에게 말하고 있을지도 모르겠구나. 그리고 나는 너희 말을 들을 수도 없고. . . ."

"그래요, 아빠! 그래요!"

"안녕, 잭." 아빠가 말했습니다. 하지만 그는 엉뚱한 방향을 보고 있었습니다. 그는 허공에 대고 말하고 있었습니다. 그러더니 그는 고개를 가로저었습니다.

"아냐!" 그가 말했습니다. "이 녀석들은 아마도 새벽까지 깨어 있었을 거야, 이야기하느라고. 그냥 좀 더 자게 둬야겠다. 몇 분 뒤에 다시 와야겠네."

아빠는 바닥 위에 책을 던져 놓고는 문 쪽으로 걸어갔습니다.

"안 돼요, 아빠! 가지 마세요!"

아빠가 나가고 문이 닫혔습니다.

"음." 제가 말했습니다. "적어도 몇 분 뒤에 아빠가 돌아오기는 할 거니까."

"맞아." 스펜서가 말했습니다. "그리고 우리가 계속 일어나지 않으면, 그는 기겁하겠지."

그것은 사실이었습니다. 불쌍한 아빠. 그는 우리가 둘 다 혼수상태 같은 것에 빠져 있다고 생각할 것입니다.

"스펜서, 우리 어떻게 하지?"

스펜서는 제 말에 대답하지 않았습니다. 그는 책을 물끄러미 쳐다보고 있었습니다.

"잭!" 스펜서가 소리쳤습니다. "봐!"

"뭐?"

"14페이지야." 그가 말했습니다. "너네 아빠가 책을 던졌을 때, 책장이 넘어갔어. 내가 방법을 읽을 수 있어."

"보여 줘." 제가 말했습니다.

"아니면." 그가 말했습니다. "내가 너

한테 읽어 줄게. 정확히 내가 말하는 그대로 해!"

"알겠어." 제가 말했습니다.

"먼저." 소리 내어 읽으며, 스펜서가 말했습니다. "당신은 몸 밖에서 아주 근사한 시간을 보냈나요? 우주와 완전히 하나가 된 기분을 느꼈나요? 이제 몸으로 다시 들어갈 준비가 되었나요?"

"네!" 저는 소리쳤습니다.

"그렇다면 당신의 몸과 수평이 되도록 자세를 잡으세요." 스펜서가 계속했습니다. "몸에서 몇 인치 정도 위에 몸을 띄웁니다. . . ."

"알겠어." 제가 말했습니다.

저는 침대 아래층으로 스르륵 날아갔습니다. 저는 제 몸과 수평이 되게 누웠습니다. 저는 그 위에 몇 인치 정도 떠 있었습니다.

"영적인 몸의 손이 진짜 몸에 있는 손과 똑같은 자리에 있도록 확실히 하세요." 스펜서가 읽었습니다. "당신의 왼손은 이마 위, 제3의 눈 위에 둡니다. 당신의 오른손은 탯줄이 있던 자리 위에. . ."

"알겠어." 제가 말했습니다.

"풍경 소리를 듣습니다." 그가 읽었습니다.

"풍경은 잊어버려!" 세가 말했습니다.

"이제, 눈을 감고 탯줄이 있던 자리에 커다란 깔때기가 있다고 상상합니다. . . ." 그가 계속했습니다.

"알겠어." 제가 말했습니다.

"자기 자신을 그 깔대기를 통해 부어 줍니다." 스펜서가 읽었습니다. "탯줄이 있던 바로 그 자리에 말이에요. 마치 모래 양동이를 부어 주듯이."

"알겠어." 제가 말했습니다.

저는 눈을 감았습니다. 저는 깔때기를 상상했습니다. 그리고 모래 양동이를 붓듯이 저 자신을 그 안으로 쏟아 붓는 것을 상상했습니다.

쉬이이익! 저는 안으로 들어갔습니다!

저는 제 몸이 다시 살아나기 시작하는 것을 느꼈습니다! 몸의 몇몇 부분이 따끔거리기 시작했습니다. 처음에는 제 발가락과 손가락이. 그다음 제 손목과 발목. 그다음 제 다리와 팔. 그다음 제 가슴과 허파. 그리고 마침내 제 머리와 얼굴이 따끔거렸습니다.

저는 제 두 눈을 떴습니다. 저는 제 몸 안으로 돌아온 것입니다!

"나 안으로 돌아왔어!" 제가 소리쳤습니다.

저는 스펜서를 찾아 주위를 두리번거렸습니다. 그가 사라졌습니다.

"스펜서!" 제가 외쳤습니다. "너 어디 있어?"

그리고 그때 저는 깨달았습니다: 저는 제 몸 안에 돌아와 있습니다. 저는 더는 몸 밖으로 나온 사람들을 볼 수 없었어요.

저는 침대 위층으로 사다리를 타고 올라갔습니다.

스펜서는 깊이 잠든 것처럼 보였습니다. 그가 그의 몸으로 돌아온 게 아니라면, 그는 어디에 있는 걸까요?

"스펜서!" 저는 소리쳤습니다. "나에게 말 좀 해 봐!"

갑자기 스펜서의 눈이 번쩍 떠졌습니다.

"내가 너한테 무슨 말을 했으면 좋겠니?" 스펜서가 말했습니다.

저는 킥킥거렸습니다. 바로 그때 아빠가 제 침실로 돌아왔습니다.

"이런, 이런, 이런, 너희 드디어 일어났구나." 그가 말했습니다. "너희 몇 시에 잔 거니?"

스펜서와 저는 서로를 바라봤습니다.

"이야기가 길어요, 아저씨." 스펜서가 말했습니다.

"그럼 이야기해 줘." 아빠가 말했습니다. "나는 작가야. 긴 이야기를 아주 좋아하지."

그래서 우리는 모두 아침을 먹으러 갔습니다. 하나 말하자면요. 딸기잼을 바른 와플이 그렇게 맛있었던 적이 없었습니다!

그날 밤 아빠는 저에게 자라고 잔소리할 필요가 없었습니다. 저는 월요일에 일찍 학교에 가고 싶었거든요.

저는 콜먼-레빈 선생님이 어서 스펜서와 저를 봤으면 했습니다.

그녀가 우리를 결석으로 표시하는 것은 절대로 안 되니까요!

Answer Key

Chapter 1

1. D "And what, exactly, is an astral body?" I asked. "It's the one inside your regular one. The one you can travel out-of-body with."

2. C "What's so great about traveling out-of-body?" "Well, it's faster than a plane. It's a whole lot cheaper. You don't have to stand in line to go through that stupid metal detector. And you never lose your bags."

3. A "Oh, I almost forgot," Dad said. "I just saw a mouse in the kitchen. So if you go in there for a snack, you may have company."

4. B "Get set for a groovy time. First, lie down with your eyes closed. Listen to wind chimes, if you have them. Be at one with the universe. Then place your left hand over your forehead. Right in the middle. Aquarian Age people call this the third eye. Then place your right hand over your belly button. . . ."

5. A And then, finally, I felt something. A little tickle against the hand on my belly button. "Seep out. . . . Seep out," I kept telling my astral body. A few minutes later I felt another tickle against my hand. This time it was like a breath.

Chapter 2

1. C Spencer was bobbing against the ceiling right next to me! He looked about the same. Only you could sort of see through him. And he looked kind of sparkly.

2. A Moving around was fun. I found out that if I breathed out, I started to sink. But if I breathed in, I rose. To go forward, all I had to do was move my arms and legs, like I was swimming. Swimming in the air. Just for the fun of it, I did a loop-the-loop.

3. D "I was thinking more like Egypt," said Spencer. Spencer had just done a geography project on Egypt. He built a pyramid out of 743 sugar cubes.

4. B "Well, we have to be back by morning," I said. "Otherwise my dad will worry. Let's pick something closer to home. How about the Bronx Zoo?" "The zoo is fine," said Spencer.

5. C I floated to the door. It was closed. I couldn't open it. I couldn't even grip the doorknob.

Chapter 3

1. A "Ladies and gentlemen," I said, "this is your captain. We are about to land at the Bronx Zoo. Please make sure that your seat belts are securely fastened. And your seat backs and tray tables must be in the upright and locked position."

2. C The zoo was closed. There were no people—except for Spencer and me. But, come to think of it, I'm not sure we really counted as people. It was very dark.

3. D "Let's go and have a look." "Zack, are you crazy?" "Spencer, we're out of our bodies." "And you're out of your mind." "But if we're not in our bodies," I said, "they can't hurt us. Right?"

4. B "He can't see us!" I said. So I moved toward the lion. Weird! Now the lion took a step backward. I went a little nearer. The lion moved back farther. "Wow! He senses we're here," Spencer whispered.

5. C "We should get out of here," Spencer whispered. "Spencer," I said, "follow me!" I backed up several feet. I put my hands together and dove toward an open space at the lion's right.

Chapter 4

1. B Spencer wanted to go on the roller coaster right away. Of course, the cars weren't running. So we decided to go on it without the cars. Going down the hills headfirst was really fun.

2. C On Broadway near Times Square, we saw a long line stretching around the block. Terminator 3000 had just opened. None of our parents wanted us to see it. About a million people get killed in all kinds of horrible ways.

3. A The popcorn smelled great. I went over to help myself to a bag. But then it hit me. I couldn't eat any. Bummer!

4. D The trouble was, the movie was way scarier than we thought it would be. I looked at Spencer. He looked at me. "I think we ought to go back home now," I said.

5. B "I think we ought to go back home now," I said. "Why?" said Spencer. "Because," I said. "I need my sleep. If I don't get home and get some sleep, I'm going to be a mess tomorrow." "You are home asleep," said Spencer. "At least your body is. The rest of you can stay out as late as you like."

Chapter 5

1. B "OK, Spencer," I said, "how do we get back into our bodies?" "There are several ways to do that," he said. "Which one should we use?" "Uh, probably the one the book says."

2. D "The book is opened to page thirteen," he said. "That's the page for getting out of our bodies. The directions for getting back in are on the next page. On page fourteen." "Well, turn the page." Spencer looked at me. "Oh, no," I said. I smacked my astral forehead with my astral hand. "You can't turn the page."

3. B "Dad!" I yelled. "Wake up!" He went on sleeping. I floated down to his head. I put my lips right up to his ear. "Dad! Wake up! We're in trouble!"

4. A "She knows about lots of weird stuff," said Spencer. "Maybe she can help. And I happen to know she stays up till dawn."

5. C We found Mrs. Coleman-Levin's room. She was in bed. Fast asleep.

Chapter 6

1. C "Mrs. Coleman-Levin! You're out of your body!" I shouted. "A splendid observation, Zack," she said. "But how did you do that?" asked Spencer. "How did you?" she said.

2. D "We don't know how to get back into our bodies," Spencer said. "We thought you might know." "I do know," she said. "Great!" I said. "Will you tell us?" "Of course not," she said with a smile. "Why not?" I said. "Because. If I tell

you, you won't learn anything. If you figure it out for yourself, you will."

3. A "Then I suggest you do some experimenting," she said. Mrs. Coleman-Levin is big on experimenting. "And I bet you'll come up with a solution."

4. B "Won't you tell us anything at all?" I asked. "Why, certainly," she said. "I'll tell you that no one who's in his or her body can see you. Or hear you."

5. D "So put your astral minds to work. Because if you're not inside your bodies and in class promptly at 8:30 on Monday morning, I'm going to have to mark you absent. And I would hate to do that!"

Chapter 7

1. A "Step two is to form a theory," Spencer went on. "OK," I said. "I have a theory that we could get somebody to turn that page for us," said Spencer. "And who, exactly, did you have in mind?" I said. Just then the mouse reappeared from under my bed. It scampered across the rug. "The mouse, of course," said Spencer.

2. B "Well," said Spencer, "maybe we can corner the mouse by the book. Maybe we can get him to run across the page and turn it over." Hmmmm. Well, it was a long shot. But for now it was all we had. "OK," I said. "Let's go for it."

3. C "These guys probably stayed up till dawn, talking. I'll just let them sleep some more. I'll come back in a few minutes."

4. A "Zack!" shouted Spencer. "Look!" "What?" "Page fourteen," he said. "When your dad threw the book down, the page turned. I can just make out the directions."

5. D "Then get parallel with your body," Spencer continued. "Float just a few inches above it. . . ." "OK," I said. I floated over to the lower bunk. I got parallel with my body. I floated a few inches above it. "Make sure the hands of your astral body are in the same place as those of your real body," Spencer read. "Your left hand on your forehead, over your third eye. Your right hand on your navel. . ."

Workbook text copyright © 2020 Longtail Books

Text copyright © 1997 by Dan Greenburg. All rights reserved.

First published in the United States by Grosset & Dunlap, Inc., a member of Penguin Putnam Books for Young Readers under the title I'M OUT OF MY BODY . . . PLEASE LEAVE A MESSAGE.

Korean and English rights arranged with Sheldon Fogelman Agency, Inc. through KCC(Korea Copyright Center Inc.), Seoul.

영혼이 부재중이니 메시지를 남겨 주세요
(I'm Out of My Body . . . Please Leave a Message)

초판 발행   2020년 6월 1일

지은이   Dan Greenburg
기획   이수영
책임편집   박새미
편집   정소이 배주윤
콘텐츠제작및감수   롱테일북스 편집부
저작권   김보경
마케팅   김보미 정경훈

펴낸이   이수영
펴낸곳   (주)롱테일북스
출판등록   제2015-000191호
주소   04043 서울특별시 마포구 양화로 12길 16-9(서교동) 북앤빌딩 3층
전자메일   helper@longtailbooks.co.kr
(학원·학교에서 본 도서를 교재로 사용하길 원하시는 경우 전자메일로 문의주시면
자세한 안내를 받으실 수 있습니다.)

ISBN 979-11-86701-59-1 14740

롱테일북스는 (주)북하우스 퍼블리셔스의 계열사입니다.

이 도서의 국립중앙도서관 출판예정도서목록(CIP)은 서지정보유통지원시스템 홈페이지(http://seoji.nl.go.kr)와
국가자료종합목록 구축시스템(http://kolis-net.nl.go.kr)에서 이용하실 수 있습니다. (CIP 제어번호 : CIP2020018832)